To

_____

From

_____

On this date

_____

WISDOM *for the*
GRADUATE

WISDOM *for the*
GRADUATE

PAMELA McQUADE
AND TONI SORTOR

BARBOUR
PUBLISHING

© 2005 by Barbour Publishing

ISBN 1-59310-644-0

Readings in this book have previously appeared in the titles *The Word on Life* and *Route 365*.

Cover image © PhotoDisc

Published by Barbour Publishing, Inc., P.O. Box 719, Uhrichsville, Ohio 44683
www.barbourbooks.com

Our mission is to publish and distribute inspirational products offering exceptional value and biblical encouragement to the masses.

Member of the
Evangelical Christian
Publishers Association

Printed in China.
5 4 3 2 1

PREFACE

You've waited a long time for this.

You're finally on your own, making your way through a great big world full of opportunity, adventure, and challenge.

This stage of life is exciting, but it may be harder than you ever imagined. For much of your life, you've lived by other people's rules, and even though they were sometimes confining, at least you had some guidelines to live by. Now you have to make your own decisions. Do you spend money faster than you can earn it, snapping up all the latest clothes and electronics? Or do you develop the self-discipline needed to live within your wages and maybe even save a little? Do you spend your free time partying or do you invest it in volunteer work or classes that will help you get ahead in your career? Do you stop going to church because your parents aren't there to wake you up on Sunday morning, or do you get up and show up on time? The decisions just keep coming.

To make good decisions, you need good information. If you're thinking of buying a particular automobile, you talk to others who own that kind of car and read the reviews in consumer magazines. If you're making a life-changing decision, or debating a point of morality, you turn to the one source of good information that will never steer you wrong: the Bible. As God's

Word, you can trust it completely.

This book, *Wisdom for the Graduate,* will point you to key passages in the Bible—passages that deal with the issues you'll face as you're out on your own. Perhaps it can help you through this crucial time and point you in the right direction as you make decisions and choices, both small and large. Get ready for the adventure of your life!

What's the Purpose?

*"And who knows but that you have come to royal position
for such a time as this?"*

ESTHER 4:14

Esther hadn't wanted to become the wife of a pagan king and the queen of Persia. She got caught in that situation and simply tried to make the best of it.

The plots of Haman, the king's wicked advisor, against her people, the Jews, thrust her into political intrigue. When Esther's cousin, Mordecai, asked her to intervene, she squirmed at the idea. Approaching the king could mean her death. Could she risk it?

Mordecai reminded her that God was still in control. Perhaps He had put her in this place to do this act. So Esther did God's will.

We know how Esther felt. Sometimes we end up in messy—even dangerous—situations we didn't bring on ourselves. We wish we'd never gotten involved. Though we went in innocently, it's backfiring on us.

In such a situation, maybe God has a purpose for us. After all, He still controls our lives, too. All we need to do is obey.

*Lord, when life gets messy, help me keep my eyes on You.
I need Your wisdom to make the right choices and to do
Your will.*

LOW ON FUNDS? ASK FOR GRACE

A poor man is shunned by all his relatives—
how much more do his friends avoid him!
Though he pursues them with pleading, they are nowhere to be found.

PROVERBS 19:7

What a sad picture! This poor guy's relatives don't want him around because he's an embarrassment to the whole family. And now his friends won't even return his calls. He doesn't understand. Sure, he's broke—but how could everyone turn on him like this?

This guy has probably become a pain in the neck. He's asked too many relatives for loans he'll never repay. He's mooched too many meals and movies from his friends. His constant cries for help have turned everyone off.

His poverty probably isn't his fault. Stuff like that just happens. But obviously his reaction to poverty has been too extreme and he has driven everyone away. He's forgotten that it's not the amount of money you have but your faith in God that's important. Some people can handle both poverty and wealth with grace; others spend all their time whining.

Father, money is scarce right now. I know things will get better for me later, but I'm a little scared. Help me survive this with good humor and hope, so those I love will never want to hide from me.

GETTING A GRIP ON A BUDGET

On the first day of every week,
each one of you should set aside a sum of money
in keeping with his income, saving it up.

1 CORINTHIANS 16:2

I n the old days, budgeting was simple. You bought a flat metal lockbox with compartments. Then you physically divided up your salary, putting one quarter of your monthly expenses in each compartment. Of course, some expenses didn't fit any category, and at least one compartment usually came up short at the end of the month. But the system gave you some self-control.

You can set up a system like this on a computer, so your bank account doesn't leak like a sieve. The important part—and the least fun—is sitting down with a calculator to figure out exactly how much money has to go in each com-partment each month. A budgeting book from the library can help. It's not a perfect system. But it will tell you how long it will be before you can lease that car.

Father, I need to get a handle on my money. I need to know where it's all going and what I'm doing wrong. Give me the patience to sit down and do this budgeting—and then give me the self-control I need to make it work.

FIND A SOLUTION

It is not good to have zeal without knowledge,
nor to be hasty and miss the way.

PROVERBS 19:2

Y
ou've got dreams and goals and energy to spare. Like
a cat locked out of a bedroom, you want to throw
yourself against all obstacles. Well, the cat never gets on
the bed that way. It doesn't know how to turn the doorknob,
after all.

But one night the cat tries another approach. He cries—
pitifully, loudly, for minutes on end—and because you love him,
you open the door and let him hog the bed. The cat has achieved
his goal, hasn't he? He may never learn how to turn a doorknob,
but he figured out a way around that problem.

Sometimes, like the cat, you just have to step back and think
a problem through. Hitting your head against a door may not do
the trick.

Father, I know what I want out of life, and I'm
determined to achieve my goals with Your help. Give me
the sense to figure out how to do this with the least
possible amount of pain; and if my goals are not
pleasing to You, put me on the right track.

Can I Get Some Respect?

The fear of the LORD is the beginning of wisdom:
a good understanding have all they that do his commandments.

Psalm 111:10 KJV

W e all need to feel we are respected. Unfortunately, respect is hard to earn when you're young. If you haven't been with a company for a few years, almost no one will bother to listen to your good ideas, let alone act on them. Some supervisors will even steal your ideas, taking the credit that rightfully belongs to you! What should you do?

Two paths lead to respect, and the one you choose determines your future—so choose carefully. The first path comes most naturally. You watch your back, strike before you're struck, and butter up the right people until you've clawed your way to the top.

What's the second path? Follow the principles laid down by the Lord. This is not the easy way. It's not a shortcut, and at times it doesn't even seem to work. But it will soon give you self-respect—the first step on the path to success.

Father, help me choose wisely when I come to life's crossroads. Give me wisdom to choose the Lamb's path, not the tiger's. Help me be someone who is respected for the way I live, not for the damage I can do.

Stay Single or Marry?

But since there is so much immorality,
each man should have his own wife,
and each woman her own husband.

1 Corinthians 7:2

Sounds like what your mother's been saying ever since you graduated, doesn't it? Some of your friends are happily married; many are determined to stay single until their biological clock approaches midnight; others are in marriages that are coming apart at the seams. You have friends who never stop trying to fix you up and others who applaud your singleness. Who's right?

You are! If you're single, that's what's right for you right now. You'll get all kinds of advice from everyone who cares for you, but never allow yourself to be pressured, either way. Marriage is an event of the heart, not a calculated decision.

When it's time for you to marry, you'll know. Suddenly, you'll want to see this one face across the breakfast table every day of your life. Marriage will no longer seem a threat but a promise.

Father, I want to be loved, but I'm not sure I want to be married. Give me confidence in my own feelings, and make whatever I decide right for me, in line with Your design for my life.

PROMISES, PROMISES

The LORD is not slow in keeping his promise,
as some understand slowness.
He is patient with you,
not wanting anyone to perish,
but everyone to come to repentance.

2 PETER 3:9

Promises come easily to us and are just as easily forgotten.

Of all the promises we make and break, perhaps the most tragic are those we make to God. "Get me out of this and I promise. . ." Every time we say something like that, in the back of our minds we can hear God say, "Oh, sure!" And yet we keep promising, for whom else can we turn to in times of real crisis?

Isn't it wonderful to know "He is patient with you, not wanting anyone to perish"? As often as we make and break our little promises, God never breaks one. Once His word is given, it's forever.

Father, help me be more faithful at keeping my word. My track record is pretty bad, but I look to You and Your promises as examples to follow.

From Childish to Mature

Don't be childish in your understanding of these things.
Be innocent as babies when it comes to evil,
but be mature and wise in understanding matters of this kind.

1 Corinthians 14:20 NLT

C hildren do not come into the world with morals. They know nothing about good and evil when they're born. Good and evil mean nothing to toddlers until their parents teach them the difference.

Our culture likes to pretend that evil doesn't exist today—that anything you want to do is okay, or that an evil person was somehow made that way by circumstances. In effect, society is saying that it's okay to think like a child.

It's a bunch of baloney. Most individuals brought up in bad circumstances turn out to be good people because they were taught to be good people. They were held responsible for their actions.

Maybe parts of our culture think it's okay to act like a child forever, to give in to every whim and not care how your behavior affects others, but that's childish thinking. Your mother taught you better than that!

Father, keep me aware of the difference between good and evil, and help me be a responsible adult.

My Life. . .My Money

When God gives any man wealth and possessions,
and enables him to enjoy them,
to accept his lot and be happy in his work—this is a gift of God.

ECCLESIASTES 5:19

Your parents probably have no more spare cash than you do. After all, your living expenses are less than theirs at this point, and they're trying to save up for retirement. Your father may have been downsized a few times, your brothers and sisters have taken their share for educational expenses, and pension plans aren't what they used to be.

That doesn't mean you can't go to your parents for help if you can't pay your rent or put food on the table. You may even have to move back in with them. But if you are making a decent wage, you need to pay your own way—and cut your expenses if you aren't.

There's no need to pity your parents or suffer from guilt when you need help. They consider you a good investment, and you haven't disappointed them. You are their gift from God— and their gift to God.

Lord, I'm not sure how financially secure my parents are these days, but I need to be independent now, for everyone's sake, and learn to handle my own money wisely.

ME? A GOOD EXAMPLE?

Let no man despise thy youth;
but be thou an example of the believers, in word,
in conversation, in charity, in spirit, in faith, in purity.

1 TIMOTHY 4:12 KJV

When someone's referred to as a "good example," most likely that person is middle-aged or older. We tend to look to those who are older than we are for inspiration, figuring they have more experience and wisdom. That is not necessarily true; there are plenty of old fools around.

Don't rule yourself out of the good example population because you're young. Being a good example has nothing to do with age and everything to do with how you live your life. You can be a good example in kindergarten, providing you don't run with scissors.

You don't have to be a Goody Two-shoes, but you should try to live your life with courage and fairness and faith. If you can do that long enough, you're on your way toward becoming a good example. A good reputation opens doors that might otherwise stay closed to you.

Lord, I'm not sure I want to be a good example. Maybe for now I'll just concentrate on doing the right thing day by day and see how it works out. Teach me how I should act.

DID I COME
WITH AN INSTRUCTION BOOK?

How can a young man keep his way pure?
By living according to your word.

PSALM 119:9

Finding time to read is hard—but why not dig your copy of the Bible out and put it where you'll see it every day? It has everything you need in it. It has plenty of action and suspense, not to mention memorable characters. If you run into something you don't understand, you can flip the page and find a new subject. If you're dealing with a problem in your life, the answers to it are in the Bible. Plus it can be read in short spurts. You can read a whole psalm while the bread is toasting.

Most importantly, the Bible will teach you how to live according to God's wishes. You can't be a good person without knowing what a good person does. Invest in a concordance, and you'll be able to find everything the Bible says about whatever subject interests you. Then you'll know what God wants you to do. Life does come with an instruction Book.

Father, when I have a question about what I should do in a certain circumstance, remind me that all Your answers are there for me in Your Word.

Preparing My Answer

Always be prepared to give an answer to everyone
who asks you to give the reason for the hope that you have.
But do this with gentleness and respect.

1 Peter 3:15

Christians should be rich in hope, secure in the blessings they see ahead. Even when times are tough, they have faith in the future.

This confuses people. "You just lost your job? How can you smile?" "Your car's been totaled? How can you be so calm?" When people have known you for awhile and see that you consistently react with hope, they will be impressed and truly want to know how you do it.

You don't have to give a long theological answer. Be gentle. Since you probably already know these people, you can tailor your answer so that you show respect for their beliefs.

You've sat around and participated in bull sessions about politics, life on other planets, and the perfect mate. The rules are the same here. Don't let the word witnessing scare you when people seem truly interested in gaining a little hope for themselves.

Father, give me wisdom when people ask me about my faith. Help me answer their questions with gentleness and respect, bringing glory to You.

Who Is the Real Me?

But let every man prove his own work,
and then shall he have rejoicing in himself alone,
and not in another. For every man shall bear his own burden.

GALATIANS 6:4 – 5 KJV

Once you graduate and go out into the world, peer pressure lessens, although you will always have some pressure from the groups to which you belong—work groups, church groups, social groups, and so on. At this point in life, though, you have more groups to choose from, and their demands are more moderate, so you have more freedom. You have the chance to "reinvent" yourself. A shy high school student can choose to speak out in a new group. A follower can become a leader, or a leader can decide to take a break.

Now is the time to become the person you've always thought you could be. Carefully choose the groups with whom you want to associate. Assume responsibility for your own actions and take pride in the way you live, "for each one should carry his own load."

Lord, now that I have the freedom to be whoever I want to be, help me make wise choices. I want to live a life I can be proud of, and I know You have something special in mind for me.

SHOW SOME ENTHUSIASM!

Serve wholeheartedly,
as if you were serving the LORD, not men.

EPHESIANS 6:7

Young people are noted for their vitality and enthusiasm. God likes that attitude so much that He promises to reward those who show that kind of wholeheartedness in their work, doing it as if they were working for Him instead of for their bosses.

Unfortunately, age and experience seem to take the edge off our enthusiasm. Some jobs just don't reward it. At first, employers welcome enthusiasm, but then it begins to annoy them. Like too much sugar, enthusiasm can become—well—just too much.

How do you strike a good balance? Look at someone older than yourself, someone well respected and successful at work, and see how that person operates. You'll see she's thorough in her work, quiet and humble, but when she speaks, people listen. They know in her own quiet way, she's working wholeheartedly.

She probably started off just like you, but she was able to rein herself in until she learned her job. If you too can learn to harness your energy productively, you'll be on your way to success.

Father, show me how to channel my enthusiasm into solid work that pleases both my employer and You.

DOES ANYONE HAVE A MAP?

There are many devices in a man's heart;
nevertheless the counsel of the LORD, that shall stand.

PROVERBS 19:21 KJV

There's nothing wrong with making plans—but ultimately, all our plans depend upon the will of God, and sometimes His will and ours are not the same. He knows when our plans won't get us where we should be, so sometimes He puts a roadblock in front of our carefully thought-out path and nudges us in another direction—while we mutter and complain about the detour.

This doesn't mean we shouldn't plan at all and leave everything to God. That would be aimlessly wandering around without purpose. We have to be flexible in our planning, though, aware that several roads may lead us where we want to be. We may not be able to see far enough ahead to plan the route, but God can, and His plans for us will never fail.

Lord, help me to be patient with all my plans and
dreams—even the ones You know won't work out the way
I think they will.

I Have Good Intentions. . . .

*Let us purify ourselves from everything that
contaminates body and spirit,
perfecting holiness out of reverence for God.*

2 Corinthians 7:1

Unless you plan to live the life of a hermit, this verse is going to give you problems. We live in a thoroughly contaminated world where it's difficult to be even a little holy, let alone perfectly holy.

Start with the most important fact, though: Your sins have already been forgiven. How do you thank someone for saving your life now and forever? By trying to be what He wants you to be. No, you are not going to do it perfectly. Yes, you will still sin. But you will steer clear of situations that God disapproves of. You will treat your body as the holy temple of God, who lives in you. You will treat others the way you want to be treated. It's a start, anyway, and this is one case where good intentions do count.

Father, I can never live my life in total holiness, but I can show my thankfulness and reverence for You in many ways. Help me live my life in a way that will reflect Your glory and mercy and eternal love.

MONEY'S JUST MONEY

Let your conversation be without covetousness;
and be content with such things as ye have:
for he hath said, I will never leave thee, nor forsake thee.
HEBREWS 13:5 KJV

It's not "love of money" to handle well what you have, investing and providing for your future. It's not even buying some things for fun. All these are perfectly valid uses of money. God wants you to prosper and enjoy your success.

But He wants you to keep money in perspective. Money is good, but other things are better. Wouldn't you give everything you have to pay the bill if your sister or brother needed a life-saving operation? If a disaster made you abandon your apartment, would you save your checkbook or your roommate?

Those are pretty extreme examples, but you get the point. An excessive love of money can put your soul in danger. It can shatter marriages, turn family members against one another, and turn you into someone you'd never choose for a friend. Think about it the next time you deposit your paycheck.

Lord, I know You will provide for me. Keep me from the love of money. I want to be someone of whom You can be proud.

A Mirror of Christ

But among you there must not be even a hint of sexual immorality,
or of any kind of impurity, or of greed,
because these are improper for God's holy people.

EPHESIANS 5:3

Once you declare your Christianity, your life is under a microscope. If you slip, all your nice words are useless. You can't shrug this problem off by saying it's not you whom people should follow, but Christ, who was without sin. You are the one who makes Christ visible to the world. If you intend to be an evangelist, you'd better have your own life in order.

Does this mean you can't witness to anyone because your own life is flawed? Of course not. It does mean you have to voluntarily acknowledge your own shortcomings, admitting you are a flawed mirror of God; your own sins come between others and the glory you're trying to reflect. When you admit that, people can see you as honest, a normal human being, then look beyond you and glimpse the possibility of their own salvation.

Father, I'm not worthy to be an example of You and Your way of life. Help me deal with my own sins in a way that will bring glory to You and salvation to other sinners like me.

Will You Be My Friend?

There are "friends" who destroy each other,
but a real friend sticks closer than a brother.

PROVERBS 18:24 NLT

Companions are easier to find than friends. They can be a little wacky, a little wild, a little irresponsible—and you might not want to introduce them to your mother. Companions come and go rapidly. They wear out their welcome or decide you've worn out yours, and it's no big deal when you part ways, since no one has any emotional commitment.

Of course, you can't depend on companions for anything. If they're in the mood they might help you move—once. They may lend you a twenty—once. But when you really need them, they'll be busy.

Fortunately, a few companions become friends. They hang around longer than usual. You find you have several interests in common and begin to talk seriously about deeper, more personal things. If you're really in tune with each other, you invest in each other, although you'd never say something like that. You'll just be there.

We all need friends like this.

Father, help me be careful in my choice of companions and
willing to be a good friend.

WISE SPENDING

Houses and wealth are inherited from parents,
but a prudent wife is from the LORD.

PROVERBS 19:14

B eing prudent doesn't mean being cheap. It does mean
being careful and thrifty. Some people are brought up to
be savers, though, while others are spenders. A saver who
falls into sudden money will still be a saver. A spender who goes
bust will still spend whatever he has.

A couple that is mismatched in their financial philosophy is
headed for trouble. This isn't something we usually think about
when we fall in love and contemplate marriage, but it should be.
After dating someone for months, you should have some idea of
how he or she handles money. You're not looking for a perfect
match. A person who is a little too cheap might do well to marry
one who spends a little more freely, and vice versa. What you
need is a person more or less like you, but different within toler-
able limits.

In the end, you and your spouse will decide what is prudent,
given your circumstances, so be sure you agree about your priorities.

Lord, help me spend my money wisely, and give me a mate who shares my
thoughts on this subject so we don't fall into the trap of arguing about money
and its uses.

WHO NEEDS RULES?

Let every soul be subject unto the higher powers.
For there is no power but of God:
the powers that be are ordained of God.

ROMANS 13:1 KJV

G od knows we need rules and regulations in society, or
all would be chaos. We hate paying taxes, but we can't
abolish the Internal Revenue Service and watch the
government default on its obligations. No one likes to get a
speeding ticket, but what would the roads be like without speed
limits and people to enforce them?

As someone once said, the United States has a peaceful revo-
lution every four years. If you are upset about the acts of a government official, get out there and vote.

God doesn't go into detail about gov-
erning authorities. He wants us to obey
the laws we have created, but other than
that, He left it up to us to form our own
government. We're all part of "the system," and
we all must obey its regulations—or change them
in a peaceful manner.

Father, I know we have a human government, so it will
always have problems. Give me the courage to work toward
peaceful change.

A FOREVER LOVE

And Jacob loved Rachel; and said,
I will serve thee seven years for Rachel thy younger daughter.

GENESIS 29:18 KJV

S uch a storybook romance! Jacob loved Rachel so much
that even seven years of service weren't too much.

When you start dating seriously and things look good,
your date seems perfect, and almost nothing would keep you apart.
Bad weather and inconvenient schedules can't separate you.

But time has a way of changing that glow. Seven weeks (or
seven months) later, when you know your date's faults better, you
may wonder how Jacob held out so long. With your dating partner, you decide, he never would have made it!

Relationships weren't made to be
worn like favorite T-shirts that are
thrown away when they get ratty.
Instead of picking on each other,
prayerfully sit down and try to iron out
your troubles. After all, Jacob and Rachel didn't have
a trouble-free life, but they shared lifelong love.

Are you looking for hearts and flowers or a love that
lasts?

Lord, I don't want to toss away relationships like old clothes. If
I need to, help me work them out.

Pass It On

*I felt I had to write and urge you to contend for
the faith that was once for all entrusted to the saints.*

JUDE 3

Feel as if no one ever trusts you?

God does.

Not only did He bring you to faith in Him, He entrusted you with the important task of passing it on to others, too.

If Christians never shared the faith, where would the good news be? Should all Christians stop witnessing, destroy their Bibles, and disobediently ignore the trust God has given them, in a short time the world would be even worse than it is today. How many people would know what God has said?

During the early Middle Ages, Irish monks on the island of Iona carefully copied the scriptures. While continental Europe was torn by political unrest and few people could pass on the Word, they painstakingly copied it letter by letter, keeping it alive. Because of their faithful efforts, we have the testimony of God's Word today.

Who needs to see or hear the gospel your life can pass on today?

Lord, I want to share Your good news today. Show me someone who needs to hear it.

TAKE A NEW LOOK

I am not writing you a new command
but one we have had from the beginning.
I ask that we love one another.
And this is love: that we walk in obedience to his commands.

2 JOHN 5−6

S ometimes being a Christian gets confusing. Pressures bear down, and your love grows cold. Spiritual winter sets in. So you start looking for something you've missed, some new trick to alter your life.

The truth is, you probably don't need a trick. You just need to get a handle on the old truth that's stared you in the face for a long time. Then you need to obey what you know.

When your love for God grows cold, take a fresh look at what He's already said. Draw close to the fire of His Word, and your life will alight.

When the cold, dull days of winter make you feel dull, too, renew your love for God. Warm yourself at the scripture just as you'd seek the heat of a fireplace.

Jesus, I already know so much about You, but sometimes I don't use that knowledge in my life. Help me bridge the gap between my head and heart.

WHERE DOES MY MONEY GO?

"Will a man rob God? Yet you rob me.
But you ask, 'How do we rob you?' In tithes and offerings.
You are under a curse—the whole nation of you—
because you are robbing me."

MALACHI 3:8−9

Billions of dollars are spent in America every year on R-rated movies. Each weekend, people throng to the latest violent blockbuster and plunk down their cash for entertainment.

Meanwhile, the view in other areas of America is hardly "entertaining." Churches can barely stay above water financially because so few people tithe, and some needy families only get help when their story reaches the six o'clock news.

Is it any surprise our nation is in trouble?

If we gave as generously to God as we do to our entertainment, imagine the people who could be helped.

God promises a curse to the nation that cheats Him, but the blessings that come with generous giving can hardly be imagined.

Let's start the blessing today.

Lord, entertainment isn't anything compared to You. Help me give to You first, not last.

Whoa! Slow Down!

Who am I, O Lord God? and what is my house,
that thou hast brought me hitherto?

2 Samuel 7:18 KJV

Who prayed this incredibly humble prayer? Israel's greatest king, the man after God's own heart—David!

By the end of his life, David, who had received so much from God, knew better than to "obey" God on his own terms. God had told the king that his son, Solomon, would build the temple, and even though David cherished this service for God, he humbly accepted God's decree.

After all, God had taken the shepherd boy and made him a king; he could also take the king and make him a shepherd again. David understood that without God he was nothing.

When everything's going fine spiritually, you may want to do a great work for God and start planning it. Though you can't imagine why, suddenly it falls apart.

Do you forge on, figuring it will all work out later? Or do you go back where you should have started—prayer and obedience?

Heavenly Father, when I want to serve You, I
need to be humble. Tune my heart to Yours, and
let me never jump ahead of Your plans.

Bottom Line: God's Word

*Beware lest any man spoil you through philosophy and vain deceit,
after the tradition of men, after the rudiments of the world,
and not after Christ.*

Colossians 2:8 kjv

We expect the world to try to disagree with us. After all, those who don't know Jesus aren't going to believe everything we do.

But what happens when people in our churches face us with ideas that aren't biblical or philosophies that owe less to Christianity than something else?

It's nothing new. God hasn't forgotten His church. The Colossians had the same problem.

People in this New Testament church fought off heresy from within. No longer were the apostles' teachings and the Hebrew scriptures enough. Among other things, the heretics taught the need for a secret knowledge and angel worship. They said you needed "something more" than Jesus.

If someone comes along teaching something "new" or different about Jesus, don't listen. God hasn't hidden anything you need to know about Jesus—it's all in His Book.

Anything else has no authority at all.

Jesus, I don't need anything "new" about You. I just need to know You better and better. Draw me close to You through Your Word.

THE GOOD, THE BAD, AND THE UGLY

These are the words of the Son of God. . . .
I know your deeds, your love and faith,
your service and perseverance,
and that you are now doing more than you did at first.

REVELATION 2:18–19

I f I'd known what I was getting into," Rita exclaimed to her pastor, "I never would have become Danielle's friend. I tried to help her out of her troubles, and all she can do is complain!"

Maybe you too have done a good turn—you gave someone a ride, only to have her constantly call whenever she wanted to go to the store, or you gave him advice that backfired. You did good with the best intentions, but now you wish you'd never done it.

When your good deeds seem to haunt you, know that God sees beyond the situation into your heart. He knows you desired only good. He'll bless you for that desire.

Though you experienced bad side effects from your good deeds, never again helping anyone isn't an option. Turn to the One who knows your deeds and do another good deed—chances are it won't backfire.

Lord, I know every good deed doesn't fall apart. Help me to reach out to others, even when things don't go the way I'd like.

My First Love

Yet I hold this against you: You have forsaken your first love.

REVELATION 2:4

Remember your first romance that gave you a glimpse of what real romantic love could be? Though it probably didn't work out, your first love sticks firmly in your mind. There was something memorable about it.

That first love probably wasn't any more exciting than the first moment you knew—really knew—that you loved Jesus. Whether you heard bells ring or just felt a quiet assurance, deep love flooded your soul. But has that first love for God turned to neglect?

If you don't spend time with your date or seek to please that special person, your relationship will show it. You'll have more disagreements than fun times. It's the same with Jesus. Though He'll love you no matter what, He won't be the overwhelming passion in your life—He'll slip into second place—or maybe third.

Has your first exciting love for God flagged, falling behind football games, the influence of a friend, your dating life, or even pizza? Get back on track. Ask His forgiveness and give Him every bit of your life.

Jesus, I don't want anyone or anything else to displace You. Be the overwhelming passion in my life.

Want Justice? Leave It to God

Woe to those who plan iniquity, to those who plot evil on their beds! . . .
The LORD says: "I am planning disaster against this people,
from which you cannot save yourselves."

MICAH 2:1, 3

"How can Mr. Raynes live with himself?" Trisha wanted to know. "He's laying off thousands of workers, after he gave himself a huge bonus last year!"

"Good luck finding new jobs," Bart added.

"It's just not fair," Louise agreed.

Later, Trisha began to see God's faithfulness. She ran into Louise in a mall and found that her friend had a great part-time job that gave her more time with her growing children. Bart had started his own successful business.

"I hear Mr. Raynes is having a hard time hiring people now," Louise added. "His company isn't doing all that well, because so many people know about some of his financial dealings. Seems he wasn't honest in other areas, too, and lost a few clients. He got just what he gave others right back at him."

Like Trisha, you may not see God working justice in your world, but hold on—He's always in control.

Thank You, God, for Your justice that never fails.

LOSE YOUR BURDEN

Then I heard the voice of the LORD saying,
"Whom shall I send? And who will go for us?"
And I said, "Here am I. Send me!"

ISAIAH 6:8

Ever wish that you could rewrite that verse to say, "Here am I. Send someone else"? When you feel overloaded spiritually, even though you'd like to comply, opening yourself to full obedience to God is hard.

Maybe, you worry, *if I give Him free rein, He'll send me to Timbuktu* (or wherever your least-favorite place in the world is). *How could I ever cope with that?* you wonder.

If you're feeling overloaded, take your burden to God and confess that you've been hanging on to it. Then drop it in His hands and run! Don't stick around to pull it back out of the hands of the great burden lifter.

Then let Him lead you as you make decisions about ministries with which you're over involved, family problems that someone else needs to handle, or commitments you may not need to take on.

Pledge yourself to obedience, and walk in your new freedom. Don't let that old burden trap you again!

Send me, Lord, wherever You want me to go. I know You'll give me the strength I need.

SPREAD SOME HAPPINESS

A cheerful look brings joy to the heart,
and good news gives health to the bones.

PROVERBS 15:30

You've heard the saying, "When Mama ain't happy, ain't nobody happy." There's a lot of truth to that saying, because one person can easily change the attitude of a whole family—whether it's the mother or someone else.

At home, a mother has a lot of emotional sway, but it's the same in a church, office, or another gathering of people. One complainer can do a lot of harm. One person with a grudge can spread it around in a matter of minutes.

As a Christian, you have no excuse for becoming a whiner and complainer. Instead of destroying an office atmosphere, brighten it up with a smile. Share some good things that are going on (or the good news of Jesus) during your lunch hour.

That way people won't want to avoid you—they'll decide you're healthy to be around.

Lord, even when I don't have a lot of good news, help me stay positive.
After all, I have the best news in the world—that You died to save sinners
like me.

THE PERFECT THANK-YOU

And let us consider how we may spur one another on
toward love and good deeds.

HEBREWS 10:24

A church member does a favor for you—something that takes him out of his way or takes extra effort. How do you respond? Can you assume that because you are fellow Christians, you don't even have to give a thank-you in return? Or do you have to give exactly as much as he gave you?

Ignoring a brother's thoughtfulness will not spur him on to good deeds. But turning a favor into a tit-for-tat situation won't make the deed any more pleasant, either.

When another Christian does something nice, thank her. Tell her what it meant to you. Later, if you have a chance to help her out, by all means do so. But don't make her uncomfortable by falling all over yourself to return the favor.

Instead, pass on that good deed to another. Eventually God evens up all this giving business and everyone benefits.

Lord, when a fellow Christian does a good deed for me, help me to be thankful, then humble enough to pass on the good I've received.

20/20 VISION

Jesus asked, "Do you see anything?"
He looked up and said, "I see people;
they look like trees walking around."

MARK 8:23–24

I f you are nearsighted, you can relate to this man. Step out-
doors without your glasses, and you may see trees as if they
were covered by water.

Poor vision isn't hard to correct. You visit a doctor and get
glasses or contact lenses. In a short while, you're 20/20.

But many of us with good eyesight don't recognize another
kind of blindness—the moral kind. Even Christians can fall
into this trap. Tempted by lust, we make excuses: *It's okay as long
as I only go so far.* Or, *Well, we plan on getting married anyway.* We
don't take a good look at the Good Book, and we ignore the
clear commands written there. Fuzzy moral vision keeps us from
knowing the truth.

Doubtful moral choices can make you feel
uncomfortable deep in your heart. Peace seems elu-
sive, and life is hard.

Feel that way? Maybe the soul doctor is trying to get your attention. Turn to the Great
Physician to clear your vision.

O Great Physician, heal my moral sight. I want to
see Your will 20/20 and walk in it every day.

TIRED? REST IN JESUS

Come unto me, all ye that labour and are heavy laden,
and I will give you rest.

MATTHEW 11:28 KJV

When you start on heavy labor—helping a friend move into his new place or digging in a garden—you work freely. It seems easy. But as you begin to tire, you set a goal: *I'll do this much, then take a rest.* Later, your muscles feel the strain, and thoughts of a break fill your mind. Finally, you just have to stop working. It's the same with emotional or spiritual work. You can't go on forever without Jesus' rest.

When you're working forty hours a week, hitting the mall after work, involved in ministry, and visiting friends on the weekend, by the time you get home, you're exhausted. Your Bible sits unused on your nightstand. Next morning, you scramble to the office, and a quiet time just doesn't seem to fit in.

Life's too hectic, you think.

Well, of course it is! You missed the first part of this verse and didn't come to Jesus.

Lord, each day I need to come to You in prayer and through the scriptures. When I'm feeling too busy, draw me with Your Spirit. I need to schedule a meeting with You.

Talk to God

But when you pray, go into your room,
close the door and pray to your Father, who is unseen.

MATTHEW 6:6

Time got away from Amy that morning, and prayer seemed out of the question. Jumping in her car, she decided, *I'll just pray while I drive.*

As she started off, so did her prayer, but soon she got caught in traffic. Faced with the choice of having an accident or praying, she kept her mind on the road. Past the traffic, Amy turned again to prayer, only to lose track once more when she saw a SALE sign on one of her favorite stores.

Sure, you can pray while you drive—maybe you should sometimes—but if that's the only time you spend with God, you won't be giving Him your best. After all, two seconds of prayer here and a minute there can't compete with solid time when God can answer you.

If you only talked to your friends while you drove, you couldn't give them your full attention, and your communication would get mixed up. It's the same with God.

Lord, I know I can pray when I drive, but there are too many distractions to make it my prayer room. My life includes time to spend with You. Show me when it is.

LOST? LOOK TO GOD

*"But as for you, be strong and do not give up,
for your work will be rewarded."*

2 CHRONICLES 15:7

How do you know what God wants you to do? If you think you know, how can you be sure you're not acting out of your own desires instead of God's? Sometimes God seems to be pushing you one way; the next day you feel as if you're on your own.

Doing God's will is a long-term project. You may start out in one direction and get sidetracked. A roadblock may suddenly appear ahead of you, forcing a detour you didn't expect. A door of opportunity you never knew existed may open right in front of you. Our paths seem to travel more like a sailboat than a powerboat. We tack from one direction to another, not making much forward progress.

Eventually you'll know where you're going. Your road will suddenly feel right, and you'll see signs of your destination on the horizon. So tack if you have to, but never give up seeking to do God's will for your life.

Father, thank You for the guidance You give me. Although my progress may seem slow, I know You will get me where I'm supposed to be.

SEEK GOD

*In everything that he undertook in the service of God's temple
and in obedience to the law and the commands,
he sought his God and worked wholeheartedly. And so he prospered.*

2 CHRONICLES 31:21

King Hezekiah was totally committed to the service of God, seeking His will and working wholeheartedly. As a result, he prospered. Should we expect anything less if we commit our lives to God and wholeheartedly follow His will?

The Bible doesn't say that Hezekiah had an easy time of it. If you read his whole story, you'll see he worked harder than today's corporate leaders ever do. There must have been days when he was sick of all the organizing, rebuilding, defending, and other chores that fall on a king. He'd solve one problem only to have six others appear.

Hezekiah wasn't perfect, either. He and the whole kingdom were punished for their pride when Hezekiah neglected to give God the glory for a miracle. He must have been a wise man to rule successfully for twenty-nine years. But remember, Hezekiah was twenty-five when he became king!

*Lord, teach me to seek Your will with all my heart, and do it
with the wisdom and enthusiasm of Hezekiah, the young king
who was rewarded for his faithfulness.*

HIDDEN REWARDS

He repays a man for what he has done;
he brings upon him what his conduct deserves.

JOB 34:11

God's rewards vary from person to person. There isn't one big, specific reward we are all competing for, which makes sense, since all our hopes and dreams are different, and so are what we consider to be good rewards.

Sometimes God doesn't just hand us our rewards—we have to find them. It's not that God is playing games with us. He just knows that a little effort on our part will make us appreciate our rewards all the more. So the next time your life seems to be all work and no fun, look under a few bushes and discover the surprises God has waiting for you.

O Lord, You care for every part of my life and know me inside out.
Although some of my rewards may be hidden right now, I am confident You
will help me find them.

A Guilty Judge?

"Stop judging by mere appearances, and make a right judgment."

JOHN 7:24

Our whole country is caught up in appearance today, almost to the point of making it an idol. We are consumed by the desire to be thin, to be beautiful, to dress with flair and style. All of these may be perfectly legitimate personal goals, but we can all too easily pervert them, try to impose them on others, and then judge everyone as unworthy who doesn't measure up.

Today the fit mock those who puff their way up the stairs. The beautiful recommend nose jobs. The tall look down on the small; those who look as if they need a good sandwich feel superior to those who have obviously had too many.

Jesus tells us to look beyond the surface, to judge actions, not appearances. We have no right to make our personal preferences the basis for judging the worthiness of others.

Father, just as I don't want to be judged by my acceptance of some popular trend, neither do I want to judge others by my own personal preferences. Keep me sensitive to the feelings of others and help me see the true person beyond the surface.

God Will Take Care of You

To the man who pleases him,
God gives wisdom, knowledge and happiness,
but to the sinner he gives the task of gathering
and storing up wealth to hand it over to the one who pleases God.

ECCLESIASTES 2:26

Wisdom, knowledge, and happiness are the rewards of those who please God. These rewards come directly from God, with no one in between. What goes around comes around, and the sinner ends up with nothing.

Sometimes life doesn't seem to work this way, but a lot goes on that we don't see, and we have to take the Lord's word for it, because this is a long-term promise.

More importantly, this verse helps us set our priorities. Our most important task is pleasing God with the way we live. If we do this, the rewards will follow. God Himself will provide us with the wisdom, knowledge, and happiness we need, and financial rewards will follow from them.

Sin, on the other hand, has no long-term rewards at all.

Father, I want to please You with my life. If my actions result in rewards, I will be thankful for them, but living my life according to Your wishes is the greatest reward of all.

LIVING LIKE A CHRISTIAN

Unto the pure all things are pure:
but unto them that are defiled and unbelieving is nothing pure;
but even their mind and conscience is defiled.

TITUS 1:15 KJV

A Christian looks at life with a lot more hope than a non-Christian. Sure, the world is full of sin, but a Christian should be willing to give everyone the benefit of a doubt. We slip, too, and it's not our job to judge others. In general, a Christian wants to see the good in everything and everyone.

Those without faith see the world as a dark, dangerous place where might makes right. Since they see everything as wicked, why should they be good? In fact, they soon come to believe there is no difference at all between good and bad—their consciences become corrupted.

It's pretty obvious which worldview is most common today. Do you have the courage to think like a Christian? You'll be in the minority. You'll be called a fool, or at least naive. But you'll be happy.

Father, I don't want to see the world through the eyes
of the unfaithful. Your world is good. You put it here
for us to enjoy. Give me the courage to love Your
world and everything in it.

WASH YOUR MOUTH OUT!

With the tongue we praise our Lord and Father,
and with it we curse men, who have been made in God's likeness.
Out of the same mouth come praise and cursing.
My brothers, this should not be.

JAMES 3:9–10

Most of us speak before thinking. It's automatic, out of our control—or so it seems. We use words today that our mothers would have washed our mouths out for using. Stand-up comedians and movie characters use these words so often that they lose all their meaning and eventually fail to shock us at all.

But the phrase "dirty mouth" has a real meaning. Would you take communion with filthy hands? Of course not. It would be sacrilegious. Would you pick up a toddler and tell him a dirty joke? You wouldn't think of it. And yet we take our dirty mouths to church and sing God's praises with them!

If we are going to try to be holy, we have to be aware of what we say, as well as what we do.

Lord, help me gain control of my tongue, so others who hear what I say will be drawn to You and not be put off by my thoughtless words.

TEMPTED? THERE'S A WAY OUT!

There hath no temptation taken you but such as is common to man:
but God is faithful, who will not suffer you
to be tempted above that ye are able;
but will with the temptation also make a way to escape,
that ye may be able to bear it.

1 CORINTHIANS 10:13 KJV

Temptations come in all sizes and shapes, from the seven deadly sins to sneaking a second dessert when you're home alone. As the verse above says, temptation is common, and God has seen them all. Even Jesus was tempted. It's not the temptation that makes you a sinner—you have to give in to the temptation to earn that label—and God is still in control of how much temptation comes your way. Better yet, as you begin to waver, He can show you how to get out of the situation. So the next time you are tempted to do something you don't want to do (or something you do want to do), thank God for His help and look for the solution He has provided for you.

Father, thank You for Your care whenever I'm tempted. I know I will never be tempted beyond what I can bear. You will give me the strength to resist.

EARNING, NOT GETTING

*They shall not build, and another inhabit; they shall not plant,
and another eat: for as the days of a tree are the days of my people,
and mine elect shall long enjoy the work of their hands.*

ISAIAH 65:22 KJV

It's so frustrating to work hard and build something you'll never be able to enjoy. Maybe you spend your days tuning up cars you can't afford to own or roofing houses that you will never be able to afford. It's not fair.

God promises it won't always be that way. His people will live long, happy lives and enjoy the benefits of their own work. Notice that the Bible doesn't say God will give His people everything they want. It says they will earn what they get.

The apostles worked to support themselves while they preached. Paul was a tentmaker by profession. As he traveled the world, he must have spent many nights inside tents he had made himself. A number of the apostles were fishermen who fed themselves through their own work on the Sea of Galilee. In order to enjoy the works of your hands, first you have to do the work.

Father, thank You for caring for my needs every day. I promise to do my part, too.

Help! I Need a Friend!

"I have labored to no purpose;
I have spent my strength in vain and for nothing.
Yet what is due me is in the LORD's hand,
and my reward is with my God."

ISAIAH 49:4

S ome days you just can't win. The suit you just got back
from the cleaner has mud on the cuff. Your cat turned
over the goldfish bowl and ate the fish. You said something at work, and the silence that followed made you want to
creep under a desk. Nothing went right all day.

Doesn't anyone care that you had a rotten day and need a
little encouragement? Well, you could call home and get some
sympathy, but then you'd have to
explain why you haven't been home
for three months.

Why not just talk it out with
God? He listens without comment. He
knows exactly what kind of day you had, and He
weeps for you. He's there, and He cares.

Even if no one seems to appreciate me, I know that You do,
Lord. In just a second, my day can become holy when I reach
out to You.

CLIMBING THE LADDER

Seest thou a man diligent in his business?
he shall stand before kings;
he shall not stand before mean men.

PROVERBS 22:29 KJV

Maybe you're thinking you don't care whom you report to, as long as the check comes every week, but experience will change your mind. Whom you report to does make a difference. A change in your supervisor often means a promotion, a chance to have your opinions heard by someone with the power to put plans in action. It can mean the assignment of real responsibility.

You can get there by at least two paths: office politics or good work. Often the political route seems to work the fastest, especially at the lower levels. Some people rise like balloons until they hit the peak of their ability and explode. They can't handle the work.

The safest way to succeed is to rise slowly but surely on the basis of what you can do. You go up a level, learn the job at hand, and prove you can do more. Then it's safe to reach for another rung on the ladder.

Father, help me learn one job at a time and build my future on what I can do, not my ability to "look good."

Keeping Pure

God wants you to be holy,
so you should keep clear of all sexual sin.
Then each of you will control your body
and live in holiness and honor—
not in lustful passion as the pagans do,
in their ignorance of God and his ways.

1 Thessalonians 4:3–5 NLT

Avoiding sexual immorality does not come naturally—it has to be learned—and there are very few teachers you can count on today. Society at large is pretty useless, issuing plenty of warnings about disease but little positive, practical advice for those struggling to lead a sanctified life.

So who is available to teach these lessons? The best teacher is God Himself, who can teach you what He expects through the Bible. Use a good concordance to look up verses about sex, love, marriage, and so forth. You can't obey laws you don't know exist, but all the laws are there in the Bible. Besides knowledge, God can give you the strength you will need to control your own body and live a pure life. Ask for His help when you need it.

Father, thank You for guiding me in all things. Forgive me when I
disappoint You, and give me the strength I need to please You.

JUST BE JUST

And what does the LORD require of you?
To act justly and to love mercy
and to walk humbly with your God.

MICAH 6:8

What does God expect of His people? That's Micah's question. Should they bring Him burnt offerings, thousands of rams, rivers of oil? Should they offer their firstborn children as payment for their sins? What will please the God who has saved them? How can they possibly repay such a debt?

The answer is to act justly, love mercy, and walk humbly with God. Whew! Is that it? What a relief!

Well, yes, it does sound pretty easy. But when you get down to specifics, it involves a total life change. In an unjust world, we are to be just. In a day when might makes right, we are to love mercy. In a life where we need to be our own public-relations person to get ahead, we are required to be humble. And while others follow the lead of movie stars, we are to walk with God.

Father, thank You for all You have done for me. I know I can never repay You with any offering less than my whole life. Help me to be just, merciful, and humble in my daily walk with You.

I'm Trying to Not Sin. . . .

I am on the verge of collapse, facing constant pain.
But I confess my sins;
I am deeply sorry for what I have done.

Psalm 38:17–18 NLT

Jesus was the only perfect person in the world. David, who wrote the verses above, was as sinful as the next man, yet God favored him over all other kings and chose his descendants to be the earthly ancestors of Jesus.

God knows we will sin. It's in our nature to do so. Not that we can use that as an excuse, but it is a fact of life we have to live with. God meant us to live happy lives, not be weighed down by an unnatural burden of sin. Jesus has accepted that burden for us. Give it over to Him, accept His sacrifice with joy, go on with your life, and try to sin no more.

Father, thank You for forgiving all my sins through Your Son,
Jesus Christ. Let me dwell on what You have done for me,
not on the many ways I have failed You.

Telling Others in My Own Way

One generation will commend your works to another;
they will tell of your mighty acts.
They will speak of the glorious splendor of your majesty,
and I will meditate on your wonderful works.

PSALM 145:4–5

There was no Internet in the days of David, no instant communication. Most people couldn't read or write. Traditions were taught to a young generation by the older generation, often through stories, songs, and dances, which were memorable and enjoyable ways to learn. The psalms and hymns of the church not only lift people's spirits but serve as teaching tools.

Perhaps you were not cut out to be a witness. The thought of speaking to another person about your beliefs may scare you into silence. But there are other ways to communicate. Can you tell stories? Can you sing? Can you dance? Can you draw? Faith, and the joy it brings you, can be communicated through many means. Offer God the talents you do have, and He will find a way to use them.

Father, show me how I can tell others about Your mighty works and pass on the faith I treasure. You know what I am capable of, and I do want to help.

Jesus Loves the Unlovable

And as they sat and did eat, Jesus said,
Verily I say unto you,
One of you which eateth with me shall betray me.
And they began to be sorrowful,
and to say unto him one by one,
Is it I? and another said, Is it I?

Mark 14:18–19 KJV

Just the kind of firm believers you'd like to have following you if you were about to face the cross, right? Twelve men who aren't even sure of their own hearts!

Told that one would betray Jesus, for a single honest moment, not one disciple—not even brash Peter—guaranteed he would never give in.

But Jesus used these less-than-confident men precisely because they recognized their own weakness. God doesn't look for self-sufficient disciples who never err. He looks for those who know they are weak and know whom to turn to—Jesus.

If you're facing trouble and feel you lack strength to stand firm, don't waste your time worrying; turn to Jesus instead. You're in exactly the right place.

Lord Jesus, I'm so weak that sometimes I don't even realize it. When I face a cross, I can trust only in You.

Hope for Those "Bad Days"

*"They have taken the Lord out of the tomb,
and we don't know where they have put him!"*

John 20:2

This wasn't just a bad hair day for the disciples. No, it was the end of the most wretched weekend in their lives.

Their Messiah had been dragged in front of the religious authorities and tried in a kangaroo court. No religious authority could sentence Jesus to death—Roman law controlled a man's life. But no Roman official had stood up to the priests. So the Master had been crucified.

Then Mary came to the tomb and found Him gone. Could a bad weekend get much worse?

Even Peter and John weren't of much help. The men merely glanced in the tomb and returned home. Heavyhearted, Mary stood crying at the last place she'd seen the Master—and saw what Peter and John missed: the resurrected Jesus.

Even on tearful days—those "bottom ten" in your life—seek Him. Sorrow turns to joy when the resurrected Jesus touches a sad heart.

Like Mary, I want to keep seeking You, Jesus. My sorrows turn to joy when I come face-to-face with You.

Make a U-Turn

"Return to me," declares the LORD Almighty,
"and I will return to you."

ZECHARIAH 1:3

Once he went out on his own, Jared didn't seem to click with the local Christian young adults. So he made friends with some fellows he met at work.

At first they seemed like good guys. Al always said good things about his family, and Don was a hard worker. But one weekend, they asked Jared to a drinking party. At first he said no. But after a couple of lonely weekends, Jared went along "just for the ride." Al got drunk, and Jared felt disgusted. But a couple of weekends later all three friends were back at a similar party.

When he went home for Christmas and got tied up again with his church group, Jared realized the danger he'd put himself in. *What am I doing?* he asked himself. *I don't like drinking, anyway.* He decided to look for some new, Christian friends, and he felt the Spirit warm his heart.

If, like Jared, you're flirting with sin, turn around today. Don't wait! The longer you stray, the harder it is to return to God.

Tempting as sin may be, help me resist it, Lord. I don't want to wake up one day and know I'm trapped.

In My Words. . .

My purpose is that they may be encouraged in heart and united in love,
so that they may have the full riches of complete understanding,
in order that they may know the mystery of God, namely Christ.

When it came to writing letters at work, Jane struggled. Nothing seemed to work. No matter how she tried, she always got more criticism than encouragement. Finally she asked Rachel, another Christian, to help her.

After reading her latest letters, Rachel pointed out that Jane was so busy using large words that her writing wasn't clear. "Say what you want to get across, not what you think will impress someone," she advised. Then Rachel turned to Colossians. "Paul didn't focus on himself when he wrote. He wrote things his readers could understand and learn from. You can make your message clear if you use this method, too."

The next time you write a letter, think first about the other person. What words will express what you want her to understand? How can you help him know your need? Then boot up your computer or pick up your pen.

Lord, when I communicate, I want to do it in a way that glorifies You, not me. Help me write clearly and lovingly.

NEED AN ANSWER? ASK GOD

Thou wast he that leddest out and broughtest in Israel:
and the LORD thy God said unto thee, Thou
shalt feed my people Israel,
and thou shalt be ruler over my people Israel.

1 CHRONICLES 11:2 KJV

David waited a long time to hear the Hebrew people remember this promise made by God. Jesse's son carried this assurance in his heart as he became King Saul's general, ran from the crazed ruler and hid in the hills, and battled Israel's enemies from afar. Though he must have been tempted to believe God had forgotten His promise, David still trusted.

The ex-shepherd boy, who had learned patience watching sheep, knew God would be faithful. But when life got stressful, he must have wondered when. David wished no ill on Saul, but he must have speculated on God's timing.

Sometimes, like David, we've waited a long time for a much-needed change—we know we need a raise in order to keep up with our rent, or we long for the end of a troublesome family problem. Like David, we don't know where the solution will come from, but we know it is coming. After all, isn't David's faithful God our God, too?

Lord, I know You haven't forgotten me. Maybe I just need to get on Your timing. Give me patience to wait for Your best.

HOLD ON! DON'T LET GO!

*Therefore, among God's churches we boast about
your perseverance and faith in all the persecutions
and trials you are enduring.*

2 THESSALONIANS 1:4

Paul commended the Thessalonian Christians on their powerful faith, which had become the talk of the Christian world. The apostle boasted about them wherever he went.

Sure, you may be thinking, *I could be like that if I lived back then. It was easier for them.*

We'd like to think that. When our own witness seems weak, we assume others have it easier than we do. We excuse ourselves, *If only I had this. . . .* Or, *If only I were older. . . .* The *if onlys* could go on endlessly.

But the Thessalonians weren't armchair Christians. They suffered and endured trials. Many must have felt that being Christian wasn't always worth it.

Do we have to struggle so much? both we and the Thessalonians have wondered. *If only God would make our lives easier, couldn't we have a better witness?* we ask.

But trials and troubles are the tools God uses to develop His greatest saints.

Hold fast today!

Lord, some days the trials come raining down on me. No matter what my situation, let me be faithful to You.

Tongue-Tied?
Talk from Your Heart

For there are many unruly and vain talkers and deceivers.

TITUS 1:10 KJV

Some of the smoothest-talking Christians are the least effective people spiritually. Though they have plenty of words and arguments and may look like they have spirituality all under control, their lives miss God's touch if they lack an obedient and truthful spirit.

Nowhere in scripture does God command us to speak perfectly before we share our faith. Neither Moses nor Paul claimed to have public speaking down pat, but how they talked didn't matter. The Lord wasn't looking for con men; He used these leaders powerfully because they were obedient.

A smooth talker may deceive people. But even the most rough-spoken person can show people truth—especially the truth about Jesus. It's not in the words but the heart. What do your words show about your heart?

Whether I'm a professional speaker or someone who hates to talk, my words need to be honest and gentle to reflect You, Jesus.

Spiritual Fitness

Commit your way to the LORD; trust in him and he. . .
will make your righteousness shine like the dawn.

Psalm 37:5–6

Even the laziest couch potato discovers energy after seeing one of those pricy fitness machines. They offer visions of a new, sleeker you.

But once you try out these tempting machines, you learn it takes commitment and consistency to get that new figure. Before long, the machine becomes a place to drop your coat—but a clothes rack would have cost a whole lot less.

Coming to Jesus is something like buying exercise equipment. All you need to be successful is right there, ready to be used. But your Christian testimony won't automatically shine out in a dark world. That takes daily commitment and trust in God. Righteousness needs to be built up day by day.

Some people's Christian walk never goes further than their stroll down the aisle during an altar call. They don't want to change their lives. Those people are expensive clothes racks.

Seek out God every day through prayer, fellowship, and His Word, and you'll become a truly fit Christian.

Lord, I don't want to be useless to You. Make me fit for Your kingdom.

LIFE ON THE EDGE

"This poor widow has put more into the treasury than all the others.
They all gave out of their wealth;
but she, out of her poverty, put in everything—
all she had to live on."

MARK 12:43–44

Doesn't part of you wish you were as brave as the widow who dropped her last coins into the temple treasury? *How would I live if I gave that much?* you probably ask yourself. *What would I do?* Scary, isn't it?

Scripture doesn't tell us the widow went home to find money waiting for her. We can't guarantee that the story had that kind of happy ending.

But we know that, whatever happened, God knew what she had done and blessed her. Doesn't He promise to bless those who give?

Faith often means hanging on the edge, not knowing all the answers. Maybe for you it isn't putting your last pennies in the offering plate, but it's putting a tithe in when you don't know how you'll pay that last bill. Or maybe it's sharing the gospel with someone when you don't know if he'll object.

That's life on the edge of faith.

Lord, I don't want to be so comfortable that I forget what life's like on the edge. Make my faith walk exciting.

Your Faithful Friend

It is of the LORD's mercies that we are not consumed,
because his compassions fail not.
They are new every morning: great is thy faithfulness.

Troubles seemed to overflow Craig. He spent more and more time on the job as his boss loaded him with work. His mom went into the hospital for tests. His girlfriend disappeared from his life. The pastor of his church resigned, and Craig wondered if anything in life was stable.

Life's challenges can hit us hard—and suddenly. One moment you have one problem you're dealing with, and the next you have three or four. *Has God forgotten me? Will He leave me stranded?* you may wonder.

Never. Compassion is God's middle name. Every day, even the lousy ones, He remains faithful.

No trouble can eat you up when you belong to God. It may nibble at your edges, but you won't be consumed.

Lord, faith isn't just emotions. When I get that empty, stranded feeling, I know it's nothing You put in my heart. I don't want to be eaten up with worry—just consumed with Your Word.

Is Your Light On?

Thy word is a lamp unto my feet, and a light unto my path.

Psalm 119:105 KJV

"Why should I read a book that's thousands of years old? What would those old guys know about modern life?"

If you haven't actually heard those words, you've heard that message from someone who doesn't value reading the Word.

The fact is, plenty of people, even those who've walked down a church aisle to commit themselves to Christ, have trouble spending time in the Bible. "I don't understand it," many complain.

But others pick up scripture, and new truths leap out at them, answering questions that have been on their hearts for a long time.

What's the difference?

Commitment. Spend regular time in the Word and seek out teaching on it, and the light comes on. Suddenly you begin to understand, and the Spirit comes alongside, teaching you new things.

At first you get out of the Word what you put into reading it. But as you get to know God better, that light burns ever brighter.

Lord, when Your Word seems dry, keep me going. I want to draw closer to You.

Get Love, Give Love

*"Those who cling to worthless idols
forfeit the grace that could be theirs."*

Jonah 2:8

After three days and nights inside a fish tummy, Jonah doubtless felt as if God had given up on him.

Separation from God's grace was painful. It hurt Jonah to know that his own misdeeds landed him in a stinky, wet, nasty fish belly. The only thing that kept the prophet disobedient was the thought, *If I do what God says, I might like what happens even less.*

Have you felt distance between you and God? Suddenly His grace seems far off, and your prayers go no farther than the ceiling, if that far.

If you're feeling apart from God, let that feeling remind you, just a bit, what it's like not to know Him. Take action to draw near Him again—confess sin, trust in Him, and obey His commands. But once you feel His grace, don't forget that He wants you to share it with others who feel trapped in a fish belly. Give His love away as freely as you received it.

Lord, it's such a blessing to draw close to You whenever I want. Help me share that blessing with others today.

God. . .
The Only One for Your Future

I will cut off. . .them that worship the host of heaven upon the housetops.

Zephaniah 1:4–5 kjv

B ut the occult is dangerous," Brendan warned his church group. "Why—"

Another group member quickly cut him off, pooh-poohing his words. Some in the study didn't want to admit that reading a horoscope was unbiblical.

Knowing Christ isn't a cheap guarantee that you can do anything you like and still spend eternity in heavenly bliss. Dabbling in astrology, palm reading, and tarot cards isn't something God ignores in His people.

Zephaniah took the people of Judah to task for a similar divided allegiance. He never said that they didn't give God a piece of their lives. They did—but they held on to Baal worship, too. They looked to the stars for answers, as well as going to the temple.

God doesn't save a piece of your life; He saves all of it. A faithful response is to give Him your whole life in return. You can't do that if you're also trying to use occult methods to see what the future holds.

You may not know your whole future, but you know who holds it. Trust in Him.

Thank You, Lord, for holding my future. I want to trust You for everything.

EVERYDAY LOVE FOR EVERYDAY LIFE

"Give us each day our daily bread."

LUKE 11:3

Getting caught up in a round of chores—laundry, cleaning, and shopping—isn't very exciting. But the work has to get done sometime, and even the worst housekeeper has to spend some time doing it.

Surely God can't have a purpose in this, we think. *There's nothing crucial to His kingdom here.*

Does God know you have to go to the cleaners, wash the car, and buy food? Of course He does. Our need for "daily bread"— and meat, and eggs, and even clean laundry—doesn't come as a surprise to Him. He provides for it all.

But in the midst of our busyness, we need to keep time for God. We can start the day with devotions, encourage a friend who phones just as we pick up a sponge to clean the bathroom, and reach out to someone in front of us in line at the grocery store.

Even dull days become exciting when you serve the Lord of the universe.

Lord, even days that don't seem to make great gains for Your kingdom are ordained by You. Help me touch others today.

LIVE WHAT YOU'VE LEARNED

Your fasting ends in quarreling and strife,
and in striking each other with wicked fists.
You cannot fast as you do today and expect your voice to be heard on high.

ISAIAH 58:4

People who fast have a real commitment to God. It takes a lot of faith to give up food.

But even an empty stomach becomes meaningless if it's done for outward show. Christians who fast and pray, yet live sinful lives, haven't drawn near God. What they're doing on the outside has nothing to do with what's on the inside, and their daily actions show that more clearly than a public fast.

Developing consistency in our spiritual lives is challenging. We can't act as if we're "in good" with God then fight with fellow Christians. We can't say one thing and do another.

Isaiah chided people who thought outward show was more important than heartfelt faith. In their pride, they probably wondered why God didn't seem more receptive to their prayerful "suggestions" about how He should run the universe.

They weren't listening to God; they were trying to run the world. Are you?

Lord, I don't want to look good to others; I just want
to know You, love You, and serve You.

Got a Clue? Pass It On!

Teach them the decrees and laws,
and show them the way to live
and the duties they are to perform.

Exodus 18:20

Everyone new to a job needs to be taught what to do and
how to do it. You have to ask some pretty stupid questions before you can even start your work. Even flipping
a burger can be done in a number of ways, only one of which will
be the "right" way. Then, once you get the procedures down pat,
you'll go and violate some unwritten law that nobody ever men-
tioned. How are you supposed to learn all this stuff on your own?

You can't—at least not fast enough to avoid some serious
goofs. You have to take notice of all these little things while you
work, juggling everything at once. If you're fortunate, you'll find
someone willing to give you some clues until you can handle it all
alone. Treasure this kind soul. Then, when you're experienced
and savvy, take a new hire under your wing and return the favor.

Lord, give me the patience I need to learn all the written and unwritten
rules of my job. Give me one friend I can trust to fill me in, and I will do
the same for another in the future.

The Sunday Priority

We must pay more careful attention,
therefore, to what we have heard,
so that we do not drift away.

Hebrews 2:1

All your life, Mom and Dad have taken responsibility for getting you to church, but that's over now. You may live miles from them or in the same town, but except for a little nagging, they can't control your actions anymore. It's on your head if you don't get yourself to church.

There are all kinds of excuses you can use, from not being able to find a friendly congregation to not feeling the need for church. It's easy to drift away once your old habits have been broken and you're living in a new situation.

But Sunday's not the same without church. There's something nice missing from your week, even if you can't pinpoint it. Maybe Mom and Dad were right, and you need to pay more careful attention to what you have heard—from them and the Lord. Maybe it's time to find that friendly congregation and admit that you need to go to church.

Father, it's so easy to drift away from old habits, even the good ones. Help me remember the warmth of fellowship, the security of being part of a congregation, and my need for You.

Be Thankful Today

Remember now thy Creator in the days of thy youth,
while the evil days come not, nor the years
draw nigh, when thou shalt say, I have no pleasure in them.

ECCLESIASTES 12:1 KJV

Right now is one of the best times of your life. You are young and strong, unafraid of the future, and eager to experience all that life will bring. Now is the time to remember your Creator and thank Him for everything He has given you. Now is the time to enjoy yourself, sing His praises, and keep His commandments.

Remember how you used to thank your mom when she gave you your favorite food for dinner or took you on a great vacation? You thanked her with your whole heart and happily obeyed her rules. The days she gave you Brussels sprouts, you undoubtedly did not thank her—or take the garbage out without complaining. It works the same way in your relationship with God. Now, while things are going well, be lavish in your thanks, because it will be harder to do as life gets harder.

Father, thank You for the joys of life I see all around me today. Teach me now, while I am still young, how to live in a way that pleases You.

LIFE: A DAILY SURPRISE

By faith Abraham, when called to go to a place
he would later receive as his inheritance,
obeyed and went, even though he did not know where he was going.

HEBREWS 11:8

Life rarely turns out as you planned. Oh, you can sit down and list your life goals for the next five or ten years. This is actually a good idea, because it helps you focus on your priorities. Just don't be surprised when you look back five or ten years later and see how far off the mark you've strayed.

This doesn't mean you shouldn't plan. Some of the best things in your life will come to you because of planning. But some of the best things will also come without planning for them at all. That's what makes life so much fun. It's a daily surprise, and you need to stride into it with faith, even if you don't know where you're going.

Father, I know You will provide what's best for me, even if I don't understand at the time. Let me walk in faith, like Abraham, confident that You know my path better than I do.

Don't Worry!

"Who of you by worrying can add a single hour to his life?"
MATTHEW 6:27

With a closet full of clothes, we worry about not having the right thing to wear. With a cupboard full of food, there's still nothing to eat. These are minor worries not based on fact, but they continue to nag at us until we go out and buy the "right" clothes or cram the cupboard with enough food to feed a small nation.

Many people have more legitimate worries—actual needs that consume every waking moment in a struggle for survival. What's amazing is that many of these people are still happy, despite their problems. How do they do it? Perhaps they've read a little further in Matthew 6, where Jesus promised, "Seek first his kingdom and his righteousness, and all these things will be given to you as well" (verse 33).

Worry wastes time because it produces nothing, while seeking God and His kingdom is always a worthwhile activity that will banish trivial worries and provide us with whatever we need.

Father, I know the rent money will be there when I need it if I concentrate on living righteously and don't let my worries paralyze me. Times may get tough, but I can make it with Your help.

WHO ARE MY PARENTS?

But if a widow has children or grandchildren,
these should learn first of all to put their religion into practice
by caring for their own family and so repaying their
parents and grandparents, for this is pleasing to God.

1 TIMOTHY 5:4

Before you know it, your parents will be old. You probably won't notice it as it happens, but one day you'll see your mother rubbing her sore back or hear your father groan as he stands, and it will suddenly hit you that they aren't the parents of your youth anymore. In time, you'll find yourself faced with having to parent your own parents. It's scary, unnatural, and lonesome.

How do you prepare yourself for this time? The best way is to keep in touch with your parents now. Find out how they feel about medical care and retirement. What do they want their old age to be like, and what don't they want? Are they afraid of outliving their savings, or are they financially secure?

Of course, this requires tact on your part, but now is the time to learn who your parents really are.

Father, I hate watching my parents grow old. Give us all the patience and love we'll need to make their later years as happy and full as possible.

WILL SOMEONE PLEASE TELL ME WHAT'S GOING ON?

He is the Rock, his work is perfect: for all his ways are judgment:
a God of truth and without iniquity, just and right is he.

DEUTERONOMY 32:4 KJV

For centuries, wise men and women have had a hard time with this verse, so it's not unusual for the average person to ask the obvious question: *If God is just, why isn't His world? Why don't the good prosper and the evil fail? Why do starvation and genocide still rage today?*

One obvious answer is that God is working with flawed materials—us. Over the course of history, we've changed the world, not always for the better. He gave us dominion over the earth, and our sin has corrupted a perfectly just situation, which does not change the fact that God Himself is still what He has always been.

Maybe the best answer to the just-God/unjust-world problem is to admit that we don't know what's going on. We're simply not seeing the whole picture. Even if we could, we probably wouldn't understand it. Some things you just have to take on faith. God is still in the world, doing what only He can do.

Father, I place my life in Your hands, certain that all things work according to Your will, whether I understand or not.

DID YOU HEAR THAT VOICE?

Whether you turn to the right or to the left,
your ears will hear a voice behind you, saying,
"This is the way; walk in it."

ISAIAH 30:21

God has not left us alone on the earth to struggle through our lives without guidance. Whether we call it God's voice or our own conscience, it is there, and it does help. We also have the freedom to ignore the voice and go our own way. There are no strings attached to us that God can pull to keep us on the path. He will tell us which way to go, but we control our own legs.

The same thing happens to parents who raise their children properly and then can do nothing but watch when something goes wrong and their children turn to drugs or crime. Imagine the pain those parents feel and then multiply it to infinity, and you will only begin to understand a fraction of the pain we must cause our heavenly Father.

Don't let the world's uproar drown out the voice you hear behind you. It's the best friend you will ever have.

Father, I want to follow Your path. Help me listen
when You guide me in the way I should go.

DAY AND NIGHT

Ye are all the children of light, and the children of the day:
we are not of the night, nor of darkness.

1 THESSALONIANS 5:5 KJV

There's nothing wrong with the night in itself. It's a time of peace and rest and relaxation, which we all need. A child of the light—a Christian—can enjoy both day and night.

Yet there is something about the night that worries us. Not many horror movies are filmed in bright daylight, and echoing footsteps behind us in the night can raise the hairs on the back of our necks. There's a sense of danger in the night that we can never completely escape. Maybe that's part of its attraction.

The trick is to be able to enjoy the night without taking it into our souls and becoming part of it. As Christians, we have seen the light and know wrong from right. We shouldn't do anything in the dark that we wouldn't do in the sunshine. We cannot belong to the night, because we belong to Jesus.

Lord, You bring sunshine into my life, where there once was darkness.
Thank You for Your love and protection at all hours of the day and night.

A Little Discretion, Please

"But now they mock me, men younger than I,
whose fathers I would have disdained to put with my sheep dogs."

JOB 30:1

Job had fallen on hard times, and the young men who once looked up to him for wisdom and advice now scorned him and spit in his face, not showing a shred of respect for someone older. In the end, however, God restored Job to twice his prior rank and power, and we can be sure the disrespectful young men soon wished they'd kept their mouths shut.

Being discreet is always wise. People in power do fall, but a good number of them climb back, too. If your supervisor at work seems to be in trouble with the powers that be, don't make the mistake of publicly turning on him or failing to show him the respect his position deserves. If you're secretly happy to see him in trouble, keep your feelings a secret. Otherwise, you not only show disrespect for one unfortunate person, you also show disrespect for his office, and people will remember what you said and how you acted.

Father, teach me how to show the proper respect for those above me, no matter what the current situation may be.

Follow the Path

"Set up road signs; put up guideposts.
Take note of the highway, the road that you take."

JEREMIAH 31:21

We all have to see the path we're walking, or we'll end up in the bushes, not where we thought we were going. Life's a pretty long road, so putting up a few mental road signs is a good idea. When you hit a crossroads, get out your ethical road map and choose your path deliberately. You'll either decide, "No, I don't want to go there," or, "Yes, this is the way."

Note that this is your road map; we each have to draw our own. You can give advice to other travelers you meet along the way, but you can't force them to follow your path. In the same way, you can't blindly follow some other traveler, hoping she's going where you want to go. If she suddenly veers off on a side road you don't know, you'll never find your way back to the right path. Be aware of your decisions and follow the way you know is right.

Father, there are so many choices I have to make in my life,
and I can't see where they lead in the end. Give me Your
guidance so I will end up next to You.

Do the
Mundane Wholeheartedly

"Whoever can be trusted with very little can also be trusted with much,
and whoever is dishonest with very little will also be dishonest with much."

LUKE 16:10

You're just starting off in your job, and nobody trusts you with very much. You do what you're told, day after day, and it gets pretty boring after a while. Where's the challenge? What do you have to do before you get to make a few decisions or enjoy some responsibility?

Unfortunately, you have to keep on doing just what you're doing now—only better. You have to master the boring stuff first, really get it down pat, and be the best "nobody" anyone's ever seen. Don't think people aren't watching, because they are. Even boring work has to be done well, and if you sleepwalk through the day, it will be noticed. But if you prove yourself trustworthy in this job, a better one will be ahead for you. At the very least, you'll end up with a good reference for your resume.

Father, when my work gets so boring I want to nod off about midafternoon, remind me that I hold the keys to my own success in my own hands. I may be a nobody now, but I won't be for long, with Your help.

Keep Your Promises

These commandments that I give to you today
are to be upon your hearts.
Impress them on your children.
Talk about them when you sit at home
and when you walk along the road,
when you lie down and when you get up.

Deuteronomy 6:6–7

Moses was trying to impress on the Israelites the importance of following God's commandments to the letter. They were constantly to keep God's laws in mind and teach them to their children, from generation to generation. The problem was, Moses wasn't going with the Israelites to the Promised Land, and time has a way of blurring memories, especially when you've gotten what you want. Nothing makes you forget the past as fast as success, and soon enough the Israelites would disregard the rules, despite all God and Moses had done for them.

We do the same thing now. We get in trouble and beg for help, swearing everlasting devotion. "I'll do anything You ask, I promise!" Once we're safe, we forget our promises.

You're human, and you will sometimes fail, but a promise is still a promise.

Lord, often I promise things I can't deliver. Make me more faithful in honoring my word, so I can be a good example and glorify You by my actions.

TEMPER, TEMPER

A quick-tempered man does foolish things.

PROVERBS 14:17

People handle anger in various ways. Some manage to push it down and continue as if they never felt it (probably giving themselves ulcers in the process). Others kick chairs in private but soon come to terms with their anger. Still others blow up and immediately feel better. We tend to react to anger the same way our parents did, for better or for worse.

In the same way, we all have different boiling points. It takes a lot to get some people angry, while others erupt at the slightest provocation.

However you react to anger, you need to maintain control. Anger makes us stupid. We do and say things we would never do under normal circumstances, starting fistfights or saying words we can never take back.

When anger takes over, we need to get away if we can't control ourselves. Go hide out in the rest room, if necessary. Shut a door behind you until you are back in control. A real man does not hit. A strong woman asserts control over herself, not over others.

Father, when I want to strike out in anger, whether verbally or physically, give me the self-control I need to avoid doing anything stupid.

THE TRUE MEANING OF MARRIAGE

"This is now bone of my bones and flesh of my flesh;
she shall be called 'woman,' for she was taken out of man."

GENESIS 2:23

Warm sunny June brings out the brides and grooms in a flurry. After they graduate, couples who want to spend their lives together face a decision-making time. *Is this the person God has for me?* each has to ask.

If you've decided to marry this June, it doesn't matter if your day is a sunshiny blue one or the buckets-of-rain sort. Though good weather may make travel easy for your guests, it isn't the most important thing about getting married. Neither is the size of your reception or the clothes you wear.

When two people unite in marriage, they're symbolizing a deeper unity. Instead of making two out of one, as with Adam and Eve, God makes one out of two. They're meant to be bound together for life.

Living out that commitment every day is more important than weather, the number of guests, or clothes. Those things last in your memory, but they can't replace a lifetime together.

Lord, thank You for reminding me of the importance of marriage. I want to make mine one that lasts a lifetime.

CHECK YOUR RESPONSE

Do not rebuke an older man harshly,
but exhort him as if he were your father.

1 TIMOTHY 5:1

That older guy makes you nuts! All you hear from him are the things you can't do, to the point where you wonder if you'll ever be old enough to walk a dog.

Some terrific people—twenty, thirty, and even forty years older than you—have positive outlooks and encourage you in most things you take on. They're joyful people you're glad to be around.

But that one person. . .

When your personal naysayer starts carping, your mind lists all the ways you'd like to respond. *I'm not a baby anymore. I have a place of my own. You know, my boss trusts me more than you do.* Hold on —long enough to toss those words out of your mind. Exploding won't improve your situation. He'll just go away thinking he was right after all. Instead, prove your maturity by treating him gently.

Timothy was a young pastor trying to lead older folks. Some didn't want to listen, so Paul advised him to talk to the older generation, not blow up.

Take Paul's advice, and they'll eventually respect you.

When others doubt my maturity, Lord, help me curb
my anger and answer with love.

THE ANSWER WILL COME

How long, O LORD, must I call for help,
but you do not listen?
Or cry out to you, "Violence!"
but you do not save?

HABAKKUK 1:2

W e'd like to think believers never suffer serious, long-term wrongs. All Christians' troubles should be minor ones; after all, don't we serve God?

When we think this way, we've created a god who's almost at our beck and call. We're acting as if we're favored ones to whom He caters.

God didn't save us to place us in an ivory tower, apart from the miseries of this world. He didn't do that to Jesus, and He won't do it for us. Anyone who's been a Christian for long can tell you we don't always get instant prayer answers. Like Habakkuk, we'll find our faith tested by a long wait.

But at the end of God's delays, He often does something greater than anything we expected. Though His response may take days, weeks, or years, it comes at the right time.

Don't limit His work in your life by failing to pray.

Jesus, You're Lord of my life, not my personal slave. Help me to seek Your will in prayer.

I Just Don't Understand!

The LORD God is my strength,
and he will make my feet like hinds' feet,
and he will make me to walk upon mine high places.

Habakkuk had a hard time understanding God—Israel was a mess, and the Lord didn't seem to do anything about it. So the prophet went straight to the source to lodge his complaints—God Himself.

After a long conversation with Him, Habakkuk still didn't understand everything God was doing. The prophet didn't have all the answers, but he'd developed trust in God's sovereignty. The Creator was in control, and the prophet had faith again.

Even when you can't understand everything God is working out in your life, can you praise Him as sovereign Lord? Can you be confident in Him and climb to the mountaintop of belief?

If not, go to Him in prayer. Share your doubts and concerns, and give Him your burdens. Like Habakkuk, in a short while praise will overflow your heart.

Understanding all You do, Lord, is impossible. But I still trust that You are faithful. What I can't understand here, You can show me in heaven.

92   WISDOM FOR THE GRADUATE

HOPE FOR THE DISCOURAGED

*"Come, let us rebuild the wall of Jerusalem,
and we will no longer be in disgrace."*

NEHEMIAH 2:17

Overcome with discouragement, the Jews who had returned to Jerusalem from exile huddled in a city open to invaders. Broken walls surrounded what was left of the city, and even its gates were burned. But no one started a citywide rebuilding project.

When Nehemiah heard of the situation, instead of hunkering down in fear, he got permission to rebuild the walls. He traveled to Jerusalem, inspected the site, and confronted the people. Encouragement and a plan were all the people needed—Nehemiah gave them both.

Sometimes every Christian needs lifting up. When job hunting gets you down, it's great to have someone show you the ropes and say something heartening. If you're struggling with sin, a seasoned Christian can share how she overcame the same temptation.

Don't let discouragement get the best of you. Reach out for help!

When I feel lower than a snake's navel, Lord, it's hard to tell others. Help me reach out for help.

DATELESS, BUT NOT FRIENDLESS

Ye are my friends, if ye do whatsoever I command you.

JOHN 15:14 KJV

Tina had more than her share of weddings in her future. Just after graduation, two friends were getting married. A week later, a cousin planned to say her vows, with Tina as maid of honor. By the end of June, Tina decided, her pockets would be empty.

But it wasn't the financial strain that bothered Tina. Her at-a-standstill romantic life was the real problem.

Three weddings, she thought, *and not a date for one of them.*

Tina wanted to share her friends' happiness, but being odd girl out hurt. It wouldn't have been so bad if there hadn't been so many weddings when she wasn't dating anyone.

Without even asking, Tina knew what Jesus wanted her to do. Shelving her own hurts, she went to the weddings and rejoiced in her friends' blessings. To her surprise, she had a great time and made some new friends—because she wasn't with a date!

Friendship with Jesus doesn't mean you'll always have a date—it means you'll always have a Friend.

When it's hard to obey Your commands, remind me, Friend, that I need to stick with You through the fun times and the tough ones.

DECISIONS, DECISIONS

I have set before you life and death, blessing and cursing:
therefore choose life, that both thou and thy seed may live:
That thou mayest love the LORD thy God,
and that thou mayest obey his voice,
and that thou mayest cleave unto him.

DEUTERONOMY 30:19–20 KJV

Y ou're moving into a new life. As you graduate, a whole world sits out there to discover.

But it's a big world. Looking at the decisions you'll face and the things that could go wrong, you may feel scared.

Life's made up of a lot of decisions—do I move here, take that job, go along with the program or break away from it? More importantly, life is made up of moral choices that have even more impact on your future.

Bad moral choices can spell death for relationships, but good ones bring them new life. Choices close opportunities to you (after all, who wants to hire a thief?) or open up new vistas.

If you're really into the Word, you know what those right choices are. They're all in the Book. Put them to work in your life, and you'll be blessed!

When I read Your Word, I see the things I should do. Give me strength, Lord, to follow through with right choices.

Sing a Song

Worship the LORD with gladness; come before him with joyful songs.

PSALM 100:2

Some music sounds good to you—and some is just an irritating noise. But you've probably found out that your "noise" is another person's "sounds good."

Church music is part of the "noise"—"sounds good" debate. If your congregation likes the "oldies and moldies" of Christian music and you like the latest tunes on the Christian music shelves, you may be tempted to hold your ears during services. Worse, those slow, dull songs may lull you to sleep.

Chances are the music you can't stand is favored by your pastor or music leader. Maybe other church members have encouraged the music director to play it. Asking anyone to change it could start World War III.

This psalm doesn't mention the kind of music churches should play—it doesn't specify classical, pop, rock music, or even Old Testament-style music. That's because the music isn't important—worshiping God is. He deserves our praise, no matter what the song is. A joyful heart can always praise Him.

Whether or not your church is tuned in to your music style, sing with all your heart.

Lord, I want to praise You, not start a war. Thank You for music I enjoy. Let me sing Your praises today.

LOOKING OUT FOR OTHERS' NEEDS

*Therefore all things whatsoever ye would that men should do to you,
do ye even so to them: for this is the law and the prophets.*

MATTHEW 7:12 KJV

Jana sat in the crowded doctor's office, miserable with a head cold and barely paying attention to her surroundings. If only she could get in to see the doctor and get home and to bed!

She barely noticed the grimacing man across from her until another patient told the nurse, "He's in more pain than I am. Please take him first."

Jana admired the woman, but guilt stabbed her heart. *I never realized he was in such pain,* she thought. *If I had, would I have done the same, even though it meant a longer wait?*

Doing good for others—especially those outside our circle of friends—means tuning in to their needs. Do we block ourselves behind a pseudo-spiritual wall and a "don't touch" mentality? Or do we open up to others, talk to hurting people, and offer them Jesus' help?

After all, that's only a small part of what He gave us.

Jesus, reaching out is hard when I get boxed into myself. Open my heart and eyes so I can help others.

A Deeper Prayer Life

My intercessor is my friend as my eyes pour out tears to God;
on behalf of a man he pleads with God
as a man pleads for his friend.

JOB 16:20–21

How do you pray for others? Is it merely, "Bless John, bless Jane"? Imagine yourself in God's shoes, listening to such a shopping list of prayer. Pretty boring, isn't it? Hearing such stuff must be harder for Him than praying it is for us. God's heart breaks when He thinks of all the blessings we could ask for that He would gladly give. But if He gave what we asked, what would that be? Are we looking for healing, peaceful relationships, conversion, or a thousand other things?

We'll never quite know how prayer works to move God's hand. But through the Spirit, who intercedes for us, we can bring the needs of friends, family, and even Christians who live half a world away to the Father. Lives begin to change, and we can praise God for His works.

The Spirit intercedes for you every day. Are you interceding for others, too?

Father God, fill me with Your love for others. Let my prayer time be a blessing to the world.

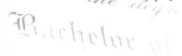

Praise Him!

I will praise you, O LORD, among the nations;
I will sing of you among the peoples.
For great is your love, higher than the heavens;
your faithfulness reaches to the skies.

PSALM 108:3–4

Some days, the praise just floats from your lips to God's ear. Whether it's your job, social life, or spiritual life, not a cloud troubles your skies. Maybe you've recently had a victory in one aspect of life, and you can't thank God enough.

Or maybe you're up to your ears in troubles, and you're stretched thin spiritually. Every day becomes a challenge. Praise seems like a word meant for someone else.

Whether you've just seen God's salvation or you're holding on, depending on it, it's time to praise Him and tell the world of His faithfulness.

Your circumstances may have changed, but God hasn't. His love never left you, and He hasn't forgotten to be faithful. If times are good, you still need Him; and if times are rotten, you know you need Him even more.

Because you trust Him, tell of His faithfulness. Even if you can't see it yet, it's coming!

How can I thank You for Your faithfulness, Lord Jesus? Even when I don't see it, I know You're working for my good.

Is It True Love?

Love is patient, love is kind.
It does not envy, it does not boast, it is not proud.

1 Corinthians 13:4

If you're involved in a special romance, do you treat your beloved as someone who's exciting to be around? Probably. But do you also show your honey God's love by living out this verse?

Dating relationships can make emotions run high, but if you're constantly impatient with a date who's never on time or are unkind to one who's having a tough time seeing eye-to-eye with a family member, you're not reflecting God's love.

God doesn't rewrite the Book so we can act any way we want in our romances. Nowhere does God say we have a right to treat the ones closest to our hearts with less respect than a chance acquaintance or a close friend. When we really love, we treat each other with extraspecial gentleness and care.

If you can't treat a date with patience, kindness, and trust, reevaluate things. Your spiritual walk may be slipping. Or perhaps this isn't a person you're suited to, and you'd be better off as "just friends."

Lord, help me show Your love to anyone I date. Don't let me make my romantic life an exception to Your rules.

Life Isn't Fair

And Joseph's master took him, and put him into the prison,
a place where the king's prisoners were bound:
and he was there in the prison.
But the LORD was with Joseph, and shewed him mercy,
and gave him favour in the sight of the keeper of the prison.

GENESIS 39:20–21 KJV

Joseph didn't look for trouble—it just seemed to find him. First, his brothers sold him for a slave. Then his master's wife lied about him and got him tossed into prison.

If Joseph was favored by God so much, why wasn't his life smooth? we're tempted to ask. He didn't deserve what he got, especially not from Potiphar's wife.

The hard fact is that the wicked of this world don't live in a vacuum—they people the earth along with Christians, and sometimes Christians get hurt by their wrongdoing. When that happens, we cry out, "Life isn't fair!" And we're right—it isn't. But it wasn't fair, either, that Jesus had to come to earth for unbelievers and die to save them.

Are you ready to be treated unfairly for Him?

Lord, life isn't fair sometimes, but I still love You and want to serve You—even if it means getting mistreated by someone who doesn't know You.

GOD'S IN CONTROL

When times are good, be happy; but when times are bad, consider:
God has made the one as well as the other.
Therefore, a man cannot discover anything about his future.

ECCLESIASTES 7:14

You can't predict the future. You can only plan to the best of your ability and move forward in faith.

So decide what kind of career you want. Work hard at it. But stay open to new ideas and truths along your path to success. Likewise, stay open to finding the mate God has for you, but don't put on a pith helmet and go hunting for one, or you'll turn romance away.

Despite all your good strategies, you'll run into a few road-blocks. Maybe your first career won't be as enjoyable as you'd expected, and you'll go back to school. Or you might wait a few extra years to meet Mr. or Ms. Right. But delays or detours don't have to end your trip.

Even your worst times aren't out of God's control. His master plan can't be circumvented. So enjoy the good days and know that the really bad ones can still lead you closer to God.

Whether today is great or out of control, I trust in You, Lord.

THE TRUTH ABOUT ANGELS

And no wonder, for Satan himself masquerades as an angel of light.
It is not surprising, then,
if his servants masquerade as servants of righteousness.

2 CORINTHIANS 11:14–15

I n certain circles, you'll hear a lot of false ideas about angels. People often use them as a more comfortable replacement for God—one that will supposedly tell them about the future but won't demand anything from them.

When you hear ideas about angels that don't agree with scripture, look out! Remember, not only are there heavenly beings, but hellish beings seek to deceive us daily.

How can you tell the difference? Look at the message the messenger bears. God's angels constantly serve Him. They don't try to take His place or detract attention from Him. They bring glory to God, not themselves.

When Satan's messengers face us, they can look good. Who wouldn't want a personal heavenly being at his or her command? But pride isn't a key to heaven, and any being that encourages it doesn't come from there either.

Lord, thank You for Your angels who watch over us. But Satan's messengers I could do without. Keep me from the pride that hides truth from my eyes.

Turning Negatives into Positives

Finally, brethren, whatsoever things are true, whatsoever things are honest, whatsoever things are just, whatsoever things are pure, whatsoever things are lovely, whatsoever things are of good report; if there be any virtue, and if there be any praise, think on these things.

Philippians 4:8 KJV

If you don't have a job yet, this isn't the time to spend your days in front of soap operas. They'll only make you depressed with their tales of sin.

It's hard not to know where life's leading you, and negatives can easily permeate your thoughts. Doubts assail your mind when you don't have a clear-cut future. But when job-hunter's depression hangs over you, spend some serious time in prayer. You may not hear a voice from heaven say, "Here's the job, in this company, at this pay," but assurance that God is working for you will fill your heart. Hang on to that assurance when Satan tosses questions in your mind!

Don't give in to negative thinking. Instead, search out positives and focus on them. Spend a few hours in the evening doing things you enjoy and that lift your spirits.

But most of all, trust the God who made you to guide you in the right path.

When I don't know where I'm going, Lord, I can still hang on to You. Show me the way.

Honoring Your Parents

Honour thy father and thy mother,
as the LORD thy God hath commanded thee.

DEUTERONOMY 5:16 KJV

S ince I moved out, my mom constantly calls me. Then the
other day, she dropped in and cleaned my apartment
because she didn't think I'd done a good job. She thought
she was doing me a favor, but I'm furious," Carla admitted.

You're stepping out, gaining independence, but Mom and
Dad don't want to let go. Though you don't want to treat your
parents disrespectfully, you are on your own. Ten years from now,
you don't want Mom stopping by to clean!

Carla's mom didn't care so much how clean Carla's place was.
She really wanted to spend time with her daughter, but when
conversation lagged, Mom felt uncomfortable and
started dusting. Once Carla discovered that,
an occasional phone call let Mom know she was
still loved. They met for lunch once in a while, and the
relationship blossomed.

You can honor your parents without doing
everything the way they do. Just treat them with
respect and keep on loving them.

Lord, when my parents and I disagree, keep us communi-
cating. I want to honor You and them.

Bear Up

*For it is commendable if a man bears up under the pain of
unjust suffering because he is conscious of God.*

1 Peter 2:19

Life is not totally just, and sometimes we find ourselves being
punished for doing what we believe to be good. God con-
siders bearing up in this situation commendable.

What does "bearing up" mean these days? In some
instances, it means continuing to live a faithful life at all costs,
including martyrdom. In other cases, it just means paying the
ticket we didn't deserve without a big fuss. Quite often, it's
easier to bear up under conditions that are severely unjust.
It's obvious that you're being railroaded, and you receive the
sympathy and admiration of others when you behave coura-
geously. The little daily injustices of life are trickier and often
harder to bear, but even then, it is commendable to persevere in
doing what you know is right.

*Father, help me bear up under unjust punishment in every
form and continue to live my life faithfully.*

BEAUTY IS SKIN-DEEP

Whose adorning let it not be that outward adorning of plaiting the hair,
and of wearing of gold, or of putting on of apparel;
but let it be the hidden man of the heart,
in that which is not corruptible,
even the ornament of a meek and quiet spirit,
which is in the sight of God of great price.

1 PETER 3:3–4 KJV

Some people would look great dressed in anything, with no makeup. The rest of us need a little help—and there's nothing wrong with looking your best. A few hours a week in the gym will not only tighten up your waistline but also leave you healthier and happier. A new dress or suit may make you more confident.

On the other hand, we all know perfectly gorgeous people whose souls live in a swamp. You may admire their appearance but wouldn't trust them to walk your dog. Their beauty is skin-deep—or less.

In the long run, it's performance that counts, which is exactly what this verse is saying. Do what you can with your outer self, but concentrate on the "unfading beauty of a gentle and quiet spirit."

Lord, I may never be one of the beautiful people the world seems to favor, but I can develop the kind of inner beauty that You prefer. Thank You for judging me on the basis of how I live, not how I look.

A Blessed Nation

Blessed is the nation whose God is the LORD.

PSALM 33:12

We don't have a state religion because our forefathers who lived under one experienced it as oppressive, limiting individual freedom. While it might be efficient to have one religion for all, we just won't line up like sheep going through a gate. It's not in our character. We're a nation of fence jumpers.

Were our forefathers great examples of godliness? Probably not. They broke the same commandments we do, just as often as we do. The fact that the press didn't follow them around with a telephoto lens probably helped their reputations, though.

It would be inaccurate to say that our country follows the Lord God today and is blessed because of it. As a political unit, it doesn't, but as individuals, we can. Those who prize religious freedom are still free to be as good as they can be, to apply religious principles to their own lives any time they want to, and to build a nation where the Lord God is free to reign in their hearts.

Father, thank You for the many freedoms we enjoy in this country. Help us build a righteous nation, one person at a time.

There's No Place Like Home

"Seek the peace and prosperity of the city to which
I have carried you into exile.
Pray to the LORD for it,
because if it prospers, you too will prosper."

JEREMIAH 29:7

Our hearts always know where our home is, especially if we're not living there. Although we may yearn to be elsewhere, we have to make do with where we are. We never have to give up the dream of returning home someday, but we do have to live in the present, and it is wise to invest in our current home. Making this town a better place to live is to our own advantage, both psychologically and financially.

Have you registered to vote in your current location? Have you found a church to attend, a doctor, and a dentist? Do you shop locally or put off buying what you need until you return to your "real" home? Do you do volunteer work? Have you made some local friends? It may be decades before you can live in the place your heart calls home. Don't waste years dreaming of somewhere else when you can contribute where you are now.

Father, show me how I can help out wherever I'm living right now.

God Knows Your Future

"For I know the plans I have for you," says the LORD.
"They are plans for good and not for disaster,
to give you a future and a hope."

JEREMIAH 29:11 NLT

We all have plans for our future, even if they're a little vague. We know whether we want to marry and have children, places we want to go, and things we hope to accomplish. Most of us are realistic about our plans, knowing some will work out and some won't. We also know our plans will change from year to year as we mature and see more of the world.

What we don't like is to have our plans blown out of the water and to have our lives take a sudden change of direction. There's nothing more frightening than losing the anchor that's been holding our life in place and being forced to start over again.

Fortunately, some of these disasters turn out to be blessings. Even when we have no idea which way to turn, the Lord knows where we're going and will keep us on the right path, even if the trip's a little bumpy.

Father, when my life suddenly turns upside down, I will trust in You to lead me in the right direction.

Dreaming. . .and Working

He who works his land will have abundant food,
but the one who chases fantasies will have his fill of poverty.

Proverbs 28:19

Two or three generations ago, young people were advised, "Learn a trade, and you'll always have work." This was during the Depression, and the advice was good, just as the verse above is good advice. Society changes, and the available jobs change with it. Today it's a good idea to know your way around the Internet and a computer keyboard. Who knows what new jobs will open up in the next twenty years?

All vocational advice is based on the same premise: Pick a job, do it well, and don't chase fantasies. This doesn't mean you shouldn't dream of a better job, but it should be a realistic dream, attainable through education or experience.

Go ahead and dream, but back your dream up with productive work, just in case.

Lord, I have so many dreams and hopes. Some will come true and some won't. Teach me the difference between dreams and fantasies, and lead me into the work You have designed for me.

FREE TO BE RESPONSIBLE

They think it strange that you do not plunge with them
into the same flood of dissipation,
and they heap abuse on you.

1 PETER 4:4

Some graduates go a little crazy once they're free of parental limits. If Dad's not around to smell their breath at the front door, they think drinking to excess is perfectly acceptable. Mom's not standing at the foot of the stairs, so it must be okay to take a date to their room. The moral police aren't in residence anymore.

It's true—they aren't. No one is going to impose moral behavior on you, short of criminal acts. You're on your own. It's a learning experience we all have to go through, and some can't handle the sudden freedom and responsibility.

Unfortunately, a lot of these moral toddlers are popular and powerful. They will heap abuse on you if you try to live a moral life. It will confuse you and may cause you to stumble, but you need to be strong. Eventually, these children will grow up and realize you were right and they were wrong. Until then, hang in there.

Father, give me the strength to follow my own values, not those of others.

What's True? What's Not?

*Avoid godless, foolish discussions with those who
oppose you with their so-called knowledge.*

1 TIMOTHY 6:20 NLT

Young adulthood is the time to decide what you do
and do not believe to be true. It's a time to question
everything, reject some old things, and embrace some
new things. It's a time that makes parents worry, because they
know you will be looking critically at their beliefs, too.

You have to do this. You can't blindly accept everything you
hear. You have to make your own decisions and be prepared to
live with them or you'll be a wishy-washy nobody.

You also have to learn discernment. That's what Paul was
warning Timothy about. Some positions must be taken on
faith. All the talk in the world can't prove the unprov-
able, so look at everything carefully before you
decide to embrace a stand; but realize that some
things just have to be accepted on faith, not facts.

*Father, no one seems to agree on anything, including faith.
Give me discernment and the courage to stand by my beliefs,
even if I can't prove they are correct.*

I Did It

When tempted, no one should say, "God is tempting me."
For God cannot be tempted by evil, nor does he tempt anyone.

JAMES 1:13

In other words, Flip Wilson was right when he said, "The devil made me do it," although he was just using the devil to excuse his own actions.

We're all tempted now and then, and when we are, we try to blame someone else. Sometimes we blame another human, our own human weaknesses, the devil, or even God. But God never tempts anyone. At the most, He might allow us to be tempted by someone else, but other than taking this hands-off approach, He is blameless.

It's not that God is unable to tempt us. There's no doubt He could do a bang-up job of it if He wanted to, but He doesn't. So when you goof up, don't place the blame in the wrong place.

Most of the time, you did yourself in.

God will not tempt you, but He will help when others do; so before you go ahead and make the wrong choice, ask for His help, which He gives freely and with love.

Father, thank You for Your care and love, which will enable me to resist the temptations that come my way.

You've Been Approved. . . .

Owe no man any thing.

ROMANS 13:8 KJV

How many credit cards did you receive in the mail before you graduated? Banks routinely send shiny new cards out to seniors, all "preapproved." Just sign the form and you're an adult, often before you have a job. Sure, the credit limit is pretty low, but in a year or so it will be mysteriously raised to a level you can't possibly afford.

Your first credit card is a rite of passage. Someone actually trusts you to pay your bills! And it's certainly handy. So accept one of the many offered if you feel you need it, but don't fall into the trap of accepting five or six of them, or you'll never be able to pay them all off when the bills come in.

If you can't pay a credit-card bill in full when it's due, you shouldn't be using a card at all. A fistful of fully loaded cards, paid off with minimum monthly payments, will never have a zero balance. You don't need that. You could take the interest you will have to pay, invest it in a mutual fund, and double your money before your credit card will be paid off. It's better to do without than to fall into the credit trap.

Father, teach me how to handle my money wisely and not spend more than I earn at this stage of my life.

THE DISCIPLINE OF ORDER

For God is not a God of disorder but of peace.

1 CORINTHIANS 14:33

The Bible is talking about worship here, suggesting that a certain amount of order should be maintained during services, but it's easy enough to see how the same idea can have wider application. After all, if a worship service can be turned into disorder, imagine what we can do the rest of the week.

Some of us are more comfortable with disorder than others. A few thrive on it, feeling it keeps them on their toes. Others can't stand disorder and feel frustrated or insecure when faced with it.

Let's face it, we're a pretty disorderly bunch. We don't have the discipline of ants or bees, and who would want it? We tend to throw our dirty socks on the floor and neglect to take out the garbage. We like a little disorder now and then.

But when it comes to work, we need order and routine. Reports need to be written on time; tools need to be cleaned and put away; work has to be prioritized or nothing will get done. Leave your fondness for disorder at home, and be as organized as possible at work.

Father, I'm not the most orderly person in my private life, but teach me how to be organized at work.

I'm So Mad! But I Still Love You

*Unto Adam also and to his wife did the LORD God
make coats of skins, and clothed them.*

GENESIS 3:21 KJV

This verse comes right after God cursed Adam and Eve,
and right before He chased them out of Eden. Smack
dab in the middle of all the thundering and armed angels,
God took some animal skins and did a little sewing. What's going
on here?

Well, that's parenting for you. How many times did your
mom yell at you, then turn around and bake cookies before she
finished her lecture? How many times did your father tell you to
be more careful with your money and then hand you a twenty
before he told you what not to spend it on?

The next time you're ready to blow up
at someone, follow God's example. Take a
break. Do a little something to show you
care for the person, and let your love
defuse your anger.

*Father, thank You for Your unfailing love when I goof up.
Your anger would be more than I could stand.*

TAKING BABY STEPS

Perseverance must finish its work so that
you may be mature and complete, not lacking anything.

JAMES 1:4

W e don't often think of perseverance as a blessing or something beneficial to our growth. We persevere because the only other options are defeat or retreat. We don't go out looking for the chance to persevere; it usually involves unpleasant experiences.

Whether or not we want these experiences, they will come. The requirements of our job may be beyond our capabilities, yet we persevere and eventually learn how to handle the work. Losing the twenty pounds we put on at college seems to go on forever, yet we lose a little every week and eventually get there.

Perseverance is tiny little steps toward a goal, not one valiant effort that solves the problem immediately. It teaches patience, planning, and working for future rewards instead of instant gratification—all things that lead to maturity and completeness.

Father, perseverance is hard work, no matter what the goal is.
Give me the patience and foresight I need to persevere and
mature.

LISTEN UP!

Rejoice with those who rejoice; mourn with those who mourn.

ROMANS 12:15

Have you noticed how short our attention span has become? Our movies have to have constant action. The same thing goes for books: Don't bother to show us the setting unless someone's lurking in the shadows. Life's too short for character development.

We do the same thing in our personal relationships. Listening is a lost art. Now when we're silent it's because we're waiting our turn to speak, not listening to what the other person is saying. As a result, the only person we truly relate to is ourselves.

That's not what friendship is supposed to be like. It takes time and patience to be a friend. You have to really listen, because often real feelings come out slowly, a bit at a time. How can you rejoice with someone when you have no idea what makes him happy? How can you mourn with a friend when you never knew her mother was dying?

Try being a good listener for a few months, and watch your circle of friends expand. You'll never be alone in a crowd again.

Father, teach me to be a good listener, someone with the patience to hear a story to its end and who really tries to understand.

NEED A VACATION?

I said, "Oh, that I had the wings of a dove!
I would fly away and be at rest."

PSALM 55:6

W hen we start sounding like the writer of this psalm, it's time for a vacation. How wonderful it would be to just fly away and rest whenever our hearts and minds were sick of it all—but we have to have our vacation time approved at work, find the "perfect" place to go, put down a deposit, arrange transportation, and buy the clothes we'll need. Sometimes it doesn't seem worth the bother or expense.

Some companies insist their employees take their vacation time, for good reasons. Vacations are about the only time we can completely relax and do whatever we want to do. Just looking forward to a planned vacation gives us a little mental rest—a "mental adjustment" that motivates us in our work.

The job will not fall apart while we're away. All in all, flying away now and then makes us better at our work the rest of the year. Enjoy.

Father, help me let go of my work and learn to enjoy the vacations I deserve,
whether I spend them at home or thousands of miles away.

Help! I'm Scared!

"In repentance and rest is your salvation,
in quietness and trust is your strength,
but you would have none of it."

Isaiah 30:15

Sometimes we are our own worst enemies. We run away from so many things that frighten us, trusting our fears more than the Lord who protects and shelters us.

Some fear commitment so much that they drive away those they love. Others are so worried about money that they never enjoy anything without first checking the price tag. Fear of losing a job keeps some from showing any initiative or creativity, which in itself can endanger their jobs.

The world is full of fearsome things, and a certain amount of caution is required, but there's no reason to let fear run our lives. Maturity and achievement come to those who know how to take a few chances. Sometimes you get bitten by a strange dog; most of the time, he licks your hand.

Trust the Lord with your life, and step out in courage and strength.

Father, thank You for Your love and care every day of my life. Help me trust You for my safety, which will let me live in quietness and strength.

Don't Look Down

You should not look down on your brother
in the day of his misfortune.

<small>Obadiah 1:12</small>

It's hard not to gloat when things turn out better for ourselves than for others, especially when we've always been the underdog. Class reunions bring out these feelings in us. The star football player turned to fat, and the cheerleaders have all had to resort to hair coloring, and we somehow feel justified by both events. These small examples of justice make us feel good.

But fortune is pretty fickle, and if we gloat, we'd better do it discreetly, because life is long, and the worm does turn. Everything will be different at the next reunion. Besides, the guy who looks like a failure now may be totally happy, while those who succeeded are miserable. You just never know. Looking down on others for any reason is futile, not to mention unchristian.

Father, only You know who is successful in life, and Your
standards are not the same as mine. Teach me not to judge
others on the basis of worldly fortune.

ARE YOU SERVING?

Keep your servant also from willful sins.

PSALM 19:13

Because you're a Christian, you want to serve Jesus. He saved you from so much, and you're grateful. Why, if you could give Him the whole world, it wouldn't be enough.

What if He asked you to give up your car, career, or girlfriend? Would you still be keen to serve? A lot of Christians wouldn't be.

We say we want to serve Jesus, but do we? Do we tell Him we'll witness, but we won't talk to our friends? Do we want to serve only behind the scenes and never give a testimony?

Only willful servants identify the gifts they feel comfortable with and try to make God use those gifts. Real servants take the place He commands.

Witnessing to friends or giving a public testimony may seem impossible. *I could never do that,* you may think.

Alone, you probably never would. But you don't have to rely on yourself. You can rely on Him to enable you to do anything He calls you to do.

Today God may call you to serve in areas that seem nearly impossible. If so, take on that task. When it looks most impossible, His grace will be at hand.

Set Your tasks before me, Your servant, Lord. I know Your enabling power will come.

WHAT'S MINE IS YOURS

"Woe! Woe, O great city,
where all who had ships on the sea became rich through her wealth!
In one hour she has been brought to ruin!"

REVELATION 18:19

Wealth! We don't often think of ourselves as having it. The other guy is usually the one who gets "the breaks," has a nicer home, or got on the "fast track" faster.

Revelation 18 seems to describe a whole city of "fast-trackers." Even those in the lowest 1 percent income bracket there could have great homes, hefty bank accounts, and drive the latest cars.

God warns us that not just personal possessions, but also beautiful office buildings, wonderful government services, and fancy department stores don't last. They're just as fragile as our smaller bank accounts, clunky cars, and condos. One hour, and poof, that city's gone.

Things don't last, but Jesus does. That's the message in the Bible's last book.

Love Him today, and you'll last, too.

Though I'd like nice things, I don't want them more than an eternity with You, Lord. No matter how much I own, make it all Yours.

GOD WORKS FOR YOUR GOOD

And we know that in all things
God works for the good of those who love him,
who have been called according to his purpose.

ROMANS 8:28

I guess we're just going to have to Romans 8:28 this," Jack's pastor commented when he faced troubles. Jack liked the expression and knew immediately what Pastor Steve meant. They were just going to have to trust that God knew what He was doing and that He remained in control. In the end, God would bring good out of the worst situation.

Are you in a situation that needs Romans 8:28-ing? Maybe you just lost your job because of company downsizing. Or your plans for more schooling fell through. Can you trust God for His timing? Maybe He has a better job that you never would have looked for otherwise. Perhaps there's a different type of schooling in your future. Wait for Him, and He'll show you the way.

When troubles come, trust God, who can work anything out for people whom He's called to serve Him. He has a plan for each believer's life.

Are you following that plan today?

Lord, I know Your plan is best for my future. Help me walk in it hour by hour.

I'm Special to God

"Though the number of the Israelites be like the sand by the sea, only the remnant will be saved."

ROMANS 9:27

God's love is so wonderful; have you ever wondered why everyone doesn't want it?

For some reason beyond our understanding, God doesn't need everyone to accept Him. He isn't in a divine popularity contest. He'd rather have a few good people to do His bidding than masses of disobedient servants.

In ancient times, God specifically chose the Jews to be His unique people. But God didn't make a rubber-stamp salvation that said, "You're an Israelite, so into the kingdom you come!" He wanted people with committed hearts. Gentile or Jew, it wasn't the background, but the heart that mattered to God.

If you know Him, He chose you out of millions of people. He wants you to serve Him because you're special to Him. There's a place for you in His kingdom, if your heart is His.

How could You choose me, Lord, out of millions of people on this planet? I'm honored to be part of Your remnant. Show me how to serve You.

Are You Lost in Anger?

I do well to be angry, even unto death.

Jonah 4:9 KJV

Sometimes God does something we really don't like. Perhaps a friend's mom dies, or a cousin's girl jilts him. It doesn't seem right, and anger fills us. *How could You do this?* we ask, forgetting—or ignoring—that He is Lord of the universe.

Jonah had seen his nation's enemies coming to God. It didn't seem fair, and Jonah flew into a snit. In fact, he was so mad, he wanted to perish.

Anger often attacks when we feel helpless about our situation. We can't imagine things changing this way, and we hate it, so we want out. Death looks better than staying here and putting up with it.

But where would death have gotten the prophet? Would it have changed what God had done, or helped Israel?

No.

We can lose ourselves in anger, or trust that God is still good and still in control. After all, the changes of a day can't alter the truth of eternity.

Lord, I don't always understand the way You work, but I need to trust in You anyway. Help me to keep my eyes on You, not my own "should-be" plans.

Pride Comes before a Fall. . . .

"And that's not all," Haman added.
"I'm the only person Queen Esther invited to
accompany the king to the banquet she gave.
And she has invited me along with the king tomorrow."

Esther 5:12

As proud Haman, King Xerxes's favored henchman, boasted to family and friends about his honors, he didn't know his downfall stood just around the corner.

Haman felt honored when the queen asked him to a banquet. But this was no celebration; it was her opportunity to report his perfidious actions to the king. Pride was deadly for Haman.

You've seen the damage pride causes on the job. A coworker gets a promotion, and before he has the new work under his belt, he's talking up his great achievements—until the day he's embarrassed as the boss uncovers all his mistakes. Or a good staff worker, jealous of a coworker, does everything she can to get her opponent out of her job—until the complainer is let go!

You're a valuable worker, but don't let pride blind you. Everyone can be replaced on the job.

When the blinders of pride surround me, Lord, open my eyes to Your truth.
Clear my vision and my heart.

CHECK YOUR MOUTH

If anyone is never at fault in what he says, he is a perfect man,
able to keep his whole body in check.

JAMES 3:2

Can you imagine never saying the wrong thing? Never telling even the whitest of lies. Not embarrassing someone by saying something clumsy. Teaching the Word and getting everything right.

Life would be perfect if you could control your tongue.

That's what scripture says. You see, what you say reflects all the things you're thinking and feeling. It shows who you really are.

Maybe we Christians have less trouble with our mouths than a coworker who swears constantly or someone who has low self-esteem and always berates herself. But perfect?

Only Jesus is truly perfect. He never gave bad advice or unintentionally hurt someone. Sometimes He told the painful truth as a warning to sinners, but He was never mean.

Need to know what to say or how to say it? Look toward Jesus. Though you may still make mistakes, you'll draw closer to His contagious perfection every day.

Jesus, I want to be nearby, to catch more of Your nature daily.

HOPE FOR THE HOPELESS

Thou, O LORD, remainest for ever;
thy throne from generation to generation.

LAMENTATIONS 5:19 KJV

For verses, Jeremiah's been crying the blues about the destruction of Jerusalem. How can he suddenly write something like this?

Judah's situation was about as bad as it could get. Conquered by Babylon, Jeremiah's nation had been wiped out, her best people carted off into exile. Those who hadn't been killed or carried away were scrounging for food.

Pretty grim.

The prophet felt despondent, but he still knew whom he could turn to. God was Judah's only hope, even if He took His time answering Jeremiah's prayer.

Sometimes life gets hopeless. The person you thought you'd marry says good-bye. A family member is dangerously ill. The job you thought you'd done so well disappears.

But you still have hope. His name is Jesus, and He'll answer your prayers right on schedule.

Lord, when You don't answer my prayers the way I
want, help me to keep trusting in You. What else
can give me hope when life looks grim?

Are You Getting
What You Deserve?

Because I have sinned against him, I will bear the LORD's wrath,
until he pleads my case and establishes my right.
He will bring me out into the light; I will see his righteousness.

MICAH 7:9

Suppose a friend had a serious lawsuit against you. Can you imagine the case coming to trial and having that friend get up to plead your case?

It hardly seems possible. When a person has been harmed, the offender should pay a price—in money, time spent in jail, or retribution. If the plaintiff pleads for the defendant, it's as if he were asking for more pain.

But what if the plaintiff held the ultimate justice and was giving you a second chance? That would be great, wouldn't it?

That's just what God does for you—He gives you another chance when you've sinned. Instead of taking pleasure in retribution, He wants to bring you into His righteousness. To make that possible, He gave His life for you.

Do you want retribution or forgiveness at work in your life?

Jesus, You'd have every right to punish me. Thank You for Your compassion that makes me holy instead. I need Your forgiveness today.

ULTIMATE WORTH

He forgave us all our sins, having canceled the written code,
with its regulations, that was against us and that stood opposed to us;
he took it away, nailing it to the cross.

COLOSSIANS 2:13–14

Credit-card bills can be such stinkers—especially if you watch them skyrocket. Pay only the minimum balance, and that debt is yours forever.

What if you got a call from your credit-card company one day saying, "Because you're our customer, we're canceling all your debt. We felt compassionate today"?

You'd probably go to a doctor to get your hearing checked. Or a psychiatrist to see if you were all right from the neck up. People don't just forgive business debts.

Paul describes sin as a business debt, with strict rules and regulations about payment and penalties.

On the cross, Jesus paid your ever-increasing debt and fulfilled those rules and regulations. At the same time, He paid a perfect price for a valueless object—sin.

He did that because He loves you.

Can you ever feel valueless again?

Lord, You gave Your life for all my empty sin and made my life valuable again. Thank You for such love.

HAVE FAITH

But Thomas, one of the twelve, called Didymus . . .
said unto them, Except I shall see in his hands the print of the nails,
and put my finger into the print of the nails,
and thrust my hand into his side, I will not believe.

JOHN 20:24–25 KJV

How hard it must have been for Thomas Didymus, the Twin. Inside his mind, he had two poles. One said faith, the other, reason. No matter what the issue, he was pulled from side to side.

When the disciples told him they'd seen Jesus, Thomas sided with reason. Though he knew Peter, John, and the others weren't the lying sort, their report seemed unbelievable. Giving it credence would take a lot of blind faith, and Thomas wasn't going to be blind.

Thomas finally ended his battle between faith and reason with the words, "My Lord and my God" (verse 28), but only after seeing was believing. Reason had to be balanced equally with faith until Thomas saw Jesus and recognized Him as God.

Are you waiting to see things God wants you to trust by faith? You'll be missing the blessing of faith.

Jesus, I don't want a divided faith. Make me whole and strong in belief in You today.

A Dream Come True

Hope deferred makes the heart sick,
but a longing fulfilled is a tree of life.

PROVERBS 13:12

Just when things seem to be going well, life can knock the pins out from under us and leave us watching our dreams fade away. Maybe you thought you'd finally found the right person to spend your life with, only to learn that your hope for love and marriage wasn't going to be fulfilled by that particular person.

It breaks your heart so badly that you give up for a while. Casual dating is safer, less painful. You back away from your hope, put it on the back burner, but it's still there; because once you've imagined a dream, it's impossible to let it go.

Eventually you'll risk loving again, and eventually you'll find the person you've been looking for—someone who shares your dream and makes it come true. Then everything will be brand-new and possible for you. You will be a new person, starting a new life with the one who fulfilled your dream.

Father, I know I will have to defer some of my hopes until it's time for them to be fulfilled. Don't let me give up on my dreams too soon, because I know You have great plans for me.

GET CAUGHT DOING GOOD

Good deeds are obvious,
and even those that are not cannot be hidden.

1 TIMOTHY 5:25

Some of our good deeds are obvious to everyone. If you regularly show up to do volunteer work, you will develop a reputation as a faithful worker. If you treat your parents with respect, the neighborhood will call you a good son or daughter. You don't do these things to impress others, but it's nice to be recognized as a good person.

Many of your good deeds will not be noticed by others, however, and you won't receive any praise for doing them. In fact, some may gain you nothing but trouble.

But that doesn't mean you should give up. Your concern and care may not be noticed or trusted, but God sees and remembers every good deed you do.

Father, sometimes I'm tempted to be as cynical as everyone else. When I'm hurt by someone's response to my good intentions, reassure me that I'm behaving the way You want me to.

KEEPING THE PEACE

Blessed are the peacemakers:
for they shall be called the children of God.

MATTHEW 5:9 KJV

Have you ever found yourself in the middle of a family argument? Maybe your dad and brother are at odds over some issue, and you step in to try to bring them back together. You offer what you think is a reasonable compromise, only to have both of them tell you to butt out and mind your own business. Often the two of them will join forces and turn on you. Well, that's one problem solved—and another begun.

The problem with being a peacemaker is that you can't totally please both sides. They don't want to come to an agreement; they want to win! So what do you do, give up? Let them fight it out on their own? In some cases, you can do just that, but in others the stakes are too high, and you'll just have to accept the fact that both sides may end up hating you for the time being when you try to be a peacemaker. It isn't easy being a child of God.

Father, give me the courage to be a peacemaker when I can help and the good sense to know when my efforts will be useless. I want to do Your will, whatever the cost.

Good Deeds for God

*"Let your light shine before men,
that they may see your good deeds
and praise your Father in heaven."*

Matthew 5:16

I f you are going to do good deeds, it's a good idea to be sure of your motivation. Are you secretly doing them for your own reputation or pleasure, or are you doing them for the glory of God?

Although doing good deeds involves action on your part, the greater portion of them also involves inaction. A light doesn't shine for its own glory. It just sits there and glows, showing the actions of others, just like a mirror doesn't physically do anything but reflect the actions of others.

In the same way, good deeds should show and reflect the actions of God, not you. It's God who gives you the motivation to do good. Even if others see you doing the acts, what they should notice is God's love, not yours. This makes doing a simple good deed a little more complicated than you thought, but eventually you'll catch on and learn to reflect God while you stand back in the shadows.

Lord, I want my actions to lead others to praise You, not me. Show me how to do this in my everyday life.

YOU CAN DO IT!

Of making many books there is no end,
and much study wearies the body.

ECCLESIASTES 12:12

I f you are starting some night classes this month, you'll soon understand this verse all too well. School bookstores are all stocked up, waiting for you to fill your arms and empty your wallet on textbooks, each costing more than a good meal for two at a restaurant with tablecloths.

The sticker shock is bad enough, but after you stack your books on your desk it will suddenly dawn on you that over the next few months you will actually be expected to read them all! Not only will you read them, you will have to remember what you've read. The sheer volume of pages waiting for you is intimidating. Just thinking about it wearies the body. How will you ever find the time?

Well, don't lose faith in yourself. You've done it before, remember? And God will be with you to help you.

Father, more education is exciting, but a little
frightening, too. Stay by my side in the next few
weeks as I get used to my new responsibilities.

WORK AND PLAY

Make it your ambition to lead a quiet life,
to mind your own business and to work with your hands. . .
so that your daily life may win the respect of outsiders
and so that you will not be dependent on anybody.

1 THESSALONIANS 4:11–12

These verses summarize the aim of all education: to be able to take care of yourself when you go out into the world. They also tell you how to act when you're supporting yourself while furthering your education: Lead a quiet life, mind your own business, and do your work.

Assignments, term papers, and demanding teachers will pretty much see to it that you lead a quiet life—relatively speaking, that is. If you're trying to balance work while getting a higher degree, you need to strike a delicate balance between work and relaxation. One way or another, the work has to get done, but you do need to take time for fun. This is a balance you need to find with God's help.

Father, help me figure out how to get everything done and still have some time to enjoy myself.

NEED SOME GOOD ADVICE?

Plans succeed through good counsel.

PROVERBS 20:18 NLT

I f you graduated last spring, you've probably had all the advice you want for a while. Parents, grandparents, teachers, pastors, and guidance counselors have been telling you what to do for the last twenty years. It's time for you to make your own plans.

You're right. You probably are ready to do your own thing. No one wants you to come running for help with every little decision. You have to make your own choices and live with the results.

That doesn't mean you won't still want some selective advice, though. This time you will seek it out, instead of having others determine what you need to know. The initiative is yours now. If you have a little money to invest, you can find your own financial advisor. A friend can tell you about a good doctor or dentist. A mentor at work can advise you on how to get ahead. The advice you seek out yourself can be even more valuable than the advice someone pushes on you without asking if you want it.

Father, help me find the advice I need to make my plans work out. I don't know everything, and I do need to know the questions I should be asking.

A PERFECT LOVE

[Love] always protects, always trusts, always hopes, always perseveres.

1 CORINTHIANS 13:7

Wouldn't it be great to find love like that in another human being? Especially the always part? Human love often comes up short of always. Sometimes it doesn't protect, trust, hope, and persevere, either. Since people aren't perfect, it's unreasonable to expect perfect human love.

Still, that's what we hope to find, and some of our early relationships fall apart when we spot signs of imperfection. Eventually we learn not to expect so much, lower our standards here and there, and find someone who's close enough. After all, we're not perfect, either, and learning to adjust is necessary in all things human.

The only place we'll ever find perfect love is in God's love for us, which never disappoints or fails. When our human love becomes a little ragged around the edges, we need to follow the model God provides: protecting, trusting, hoping, and persevering over everything until our love becomes as perfect as we can make it.

Father, our love should be a small reflection of Your love. Though I know it will never be perfect, I will give it my all.

FEAR VS. ANXIETY

Cast all your anxiety on him because he cares for you.

1 PETER 5:7

Have you discovered the difference between fear and anxiety yet? They're not the same. For one thing, fear is productive. Fear is that heart-thumping moment when you know it could all be over. The car that appears over the hill while you're passing another car causes a stab of fear, which in turn gets you back into the right-hand lane as fast as possible. Fear can be dealt with by an action you can take. Most of the time, fear helps you save yourself.

Anxiety is never productive. There is no immediate danger in sight, just a vague, overpowering feeling of impending disaster. Anxiety over car accidents may keep you out of cars, but it never teaches you to be a good driver. Anxiety paralyzes you, takes you out of the action altogether. It's a useless emotion that cripples a perfectly good life.

The Bible tells us to shun anxiety, to throw it all on God. There's enough in the world that deserves our fear, but nothing in the world should make us anxious.

Father, when anxiety takes hold of me and paralyzes me, teach me to give it over to You.

Nothing Is Too Hard. . . .

Apply your heart to instruction
and your ears to words of knowledge.

PROVERBS 23:12

Everyone looks back on high school and college days as days of carefree fun. Of course, that's because additional cares and responsibilities follow the school years, and sometimes catching the 7:00 a.m. train makes sitting in a classroom seem like a piece of cake.

The truth is, learning is hard work. It's not half as carefree as we remember it being. Names, dates, equations, philosophies, term papers, and unreasonably high grade curves give students a lot of grief. All that knowledge doesn't just flow into your brain and stick. If you're juggling coursework for a higher degree with work responsibilities, you're probably realizing that fact all over again.

Don't be discouraged, though. No matter what challenges life brings you, your heavenly Father is always by your side, waiting to help you out.

Father, remind me today that nothing is too hard for me when You are by my side.

Our Heavenly Daddy

The eternal God is thy refuge,
and underneath are the everlasting arms.

DEUTERONOMY 33:27 KJV

Sometimes we think of God as an avenger, punisher, and slayer of the unrighteous—someone we'd better not cross. The Old Testament, read too hastily, often gives us that idea, with all its curses, fires, and destroyed nations.

And yet, right there in Deuteronomy is this verse, with its loving promise. God is also our refuge, the One we can always run to. He protects us from bullies, just like our big brother did. He kisses our wounds and makes them better, like Mom. He opens His arms—His everlasting arms—and protects us from those who would hurt us, just like Dad.

Whenever we're far from home, struggling to make our way in a cutthroat world, God will be there for us. He's never too busy to help. His lap is never too full for one more lost kid. He never fails to comfort and protect.

We don't deserve this much love. We can't even begin to imagine it. And yet it's there for us anytime we need it.

Father, thank You for letting me climb into Your everlasting arms anytime I need to, for saving my life anytime it needs it, for being my Father.

A No-Fail Plan

A righteous man may have many troubles,
but the LORD delivers him from them all.

PSALM 34:19

Being righteous is no guarantee of a trouble-free life. As long as we're human, we'll have problems, whether we bring them on ourselves or have them thrust upon us. In addition to poverty, wars, and famine, lots of other problems can bring us down.

If we are righteous, God promises to deliver us from all our problems, but He does it His way, in His time, and we usually get a little impatient. Some of our troubles never seem to leave us. We may even die surrounded by them, waiting until our last breath to be delivered from them. Has God forgotten us? Why are we still suffering?

We don't know why or when or how. We just don't know. We can't see into the mind of God; we can't imagine His plans. We might not even recognize His deliverance when it does come. All we can do is trust Him and know He never fails to keep His promises. But He never promised we'd totally understand in this lifetime.

Father, when troubles surround me, help me trust in Your promises and never give up hope.

It's Your Choice

Little children, let no man deceive you.

1 John 3:7 KJV

I t's easy enough to go astray with no help at all. At least then we only have ourselves to blame. But it gets more complicated when others are involved. Is your roommate to blame when the two of you go out for a night on the town and you overdo it? Did he lead you astray, or did you follow along with no encouragement at all?

There are plenty of people out there willing and able to lead you off in the wrong direction. Indeed, finding someone who wants to lead you in the right direction is pretty hard. But who is truly responsible when you fall? Certainly not God, and probably no other human being. The verse above says do not let anyone lead you astray. There's a choice involved, and it's up to you to make the final decision.

Father, give me the courage not to be a blind follower of others. Instead, help me see where others are heading, so I can get off the wrong path in time and follow Your way.

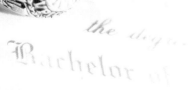

Moving Forward, Falling Back

For our backsliding is great; we have sinned against you.

JEREMIAH 14:7

Choosing the moral way certainly leads to an interesting life. One day, you feel that you've got it down pat. You know where you're going and are zipping right along on the highway to heaven. The next day, you're up to your axles in mud, going nowhere at all or being towed back to some intersection you passed years ago.

Backsliding is a devastating experience. You'd licked that problem. There were plenty of others to work on, but that particular one was behind you forever (you thought). But there it is again, standing in the middle of the road and mocking you. Maybe it'll be easier to get past it this time, but what a waste of effort.

Even when we know that God has forgiven our sins, we still get angry at our failures. They hurt our egos. When we backslide, however, the only thing we can do is confess our failure, accept God's forgiveness, and get back on the road again. It's a long journey, and there's no point in wallowing in the mud.

Father, thank You for Your forgiveness when I lose my way. I can never be the person I want to be without Your help and encouragement.

CAN YOU KEEP A SECRET?

A gossip betrays a confidence;
so avoid a man who talks too much.

PROVERBS 20:19

Have you noticed that the more you talk, the greater the chance that you'll goof things up? You say the wrong thing to the wrong person, including some things you never meant to say at all. We often do this when we're under pressure of some kind. To avoid seeming stuck-up, we say the first thing that comes to mind, only to hear ourselves talking about some deep, dark secret we weren't supposed to know about. To fit in with the crowd, we often say things we know are untrue or improper. Our tongues are in overdrive, but our brains are on hold.

Fear does this to us—fear of being left out, of being thought stupid. We feel that if we talk fast enough, others will overlook our faults and be lulled into acceptance by our silver tongues, so we let the words tumble out, only to find we've sabotaged ourselves.

The next time you feel pressured to blurt out a confidence, excuse yourself for a minute until the temptation passes. Two minutes of silence are worth far more than one minute of foolishness.

Father, teach me to guard my tongue when nervousness makes me want to ramble on.

THE HEART OF THE MATTER

Charm is deceptive, and beauty is fleeting;
but a woman who fears the LORD is to be praised.

PROVERBS 31:30

This verse applies equally to men and women and should always be kept in mind during the dating years. Sure, everyone wants to date charming, beautiful people. Even those who are less than charming or beautiful themselves hope to connect with someone who qualifies.

But you can't choose a spouse on the basis of charm and looks alone. Neither can you rule out others on the basis of a lack of charm and beauty. Take a long, hard look in the mirror, and then picture what you will look like in ten or twenty years. Don't you still hope to find someone to love the real you? Can you expect this from others and not give it to them in return?

Charm and beauty are simply attractors. Their job is to get someone's attention and give you the chance to win him or her. They're like the beautiful flower that makes it possible for a plant to reproduce, then fades away. It's the whole plant that's important, not just the flower.

Father, teach me to look beyond the surface and fall in love
with a whole person, not just a pretty face.

REJECT IDOLS

"If we are thrown into the blazing furnace,
the God we serve is able to save us from it,
and he will rescue us from your hand, O king.
But even if he does not, we want you to know, O king,
that we will not serve your gods or worship
the image of gold you have set up."

DANIEL 3:17–18

Shadrach, Meshach, and Abednego didn't mess around, even when threatened by a king. Notice their tone of voice in these verses. They're polite, but they're sure not groveling.

Don't be fooled—we, too, are asked to worship idols every day. They aren't gold statues, and no one expects us to physically fall down before them, but they do influence our lives.

There's the idol of the bottom line that's worshipped by corporations. Mess with that one, and you're out of work. There's the idol of personal beauty that steals our time, effort, and money and urges us to admire the unadmirable. There's the idol of personal wealth that convinces us to work at jobs we hate and act more aggressively than we should.

What are your personal idols? Can you be as strong as Shadrach, Meshach, and Abednego and reject them?

Father, show me the idols of my heart and deliver me from them.

Find a Job

For we hear that there are some which walk among you disorderly,
working not at all, but are busybodies.
Now them that are such we command and exhort by our LORD Jesus
Christ, that with quietness they work, and eat their own bread.

2 Thessalonians 3:11–12 kjv

Some people get away without working. A lot of them are young, still living at home, and being supported by their parents until they "find themselves." Well, what they need to find is a job. Any job.

There will always be those who are legitimately unable to support themselves, but we're not talking about them. We're talking about those who can't earn what they think they "deserve," those who are above taking a minimum-wage job and working their way up a rung at a time. Others can't find a "fulfilling" job. Ask your grandparents if their jobs were fulfilling, and give them a good laugh. Sometimes just putting bread on the table is fulfillment enough.

God gave most of us the basic equipment necessary to earn a living: two hands, a strong back, and a nimble brain. You're not going to start at the top, but until you start somewhere, you're going nowhere.

Father, thank You for giving me the ability to provide for myself. The rest is up to me now.

Don't Get Carried Away

Do not be carried away by all kinds of strange teachings.

We're a curious species, always eager to look into something new and exciting. That's good. Without our urge to explore, we'd still be dropping like flies from diseases. Without transportation, our world would consist of the five- or ten-mile radius around our homes. We explore, learn, and improve ourselves.

As we do, we'll run into some pretty strange teachings. Some of them may prove worthy with time, but others will turn out to be shams or simple mistakes or misunderstandings. It's confusing. Look at the whole field of alternative medicine today. Some of its approaches may prove to be valid, while others will be foolishness. Right now, even traditional medicine keeps giving us contradictory advice: eat fish. . .no, don't; butter or margarine? Zinc for colds or vitamin C or chicken soup?

The best advice is found in the verse above: Don't get carried away with anything. Give time and experience the chance to clarify a new discovery before you wrap your life up in it. Be cautious of new teachings, but keep an open mind.

Father, knowledge is increasing faster than our brains can sort out fact from fiction. Give me a level head.

152 WISDOM FOR THE GRADUATE

FRIENDS FOREVER

A righteous man is cautious in friendship.

PROVERBS 12:26

We need friends at all stages of our lives, but especially when we're young and still trying to figure life out. Friends give us other viewpoints to consider. When we share experiences, we can save ourselves a great deal of time by avoiding some of our friends' mistakes. We trust friends, often more than we trust our parents, because we have more in common with them.

Which is exactly why we need to be cautious in choosing our friends. Sometimes they betray us. Sometimes we discover they're not going in the direction we want to go, and it's hard to break up a friendship when we make this discovery.

Friendships also change as they mature, and sometimes these changes will hurt. Friends grow apart and then reconnect as time goes by, in a sort of cyclical flow—acquaintance, friend, acquaintance, friend again. A good friendship can tolerate these changes and grow stronger with each fluctuation. Choose your friends cautiously, and when you find a good one, hang onto him or her throughout your life.

Father, help me choose my friends with care, and treasure those who stick by me through all life's ups and downs.

The Work of the Spirit

For the word of God is living and active.
Sharper than any double-edged sword, it penetrates even to
dividing soul and spirit, joints and marrow;
it judges the thoughts and attitudes of the heart.

Hebrews 4:12

Have you ever picked up your devotional, read the scripture, and felt as if God had written that verse especially for you? It went right to your heart because you were living out that verse.

The Bible isn't like any other book. Though you might enjoy a novel or learn a lot from a how-to book, neither reaches deep inside your soul the way scripture does. The Word of God gets straight inside you and cuts to the truth in an instant. The Spirit can wield it like a sword, cutting sin out of your life.

But you have to hold still while God uses that sword; otherwise you can get all cut up. You'll leave a painful quiet time without the benefit of having the cancer of sin removed. Let God have His way with you, and though the sword might hurt at first, healing can come rapidly.

By the end of your prayers, you might feel whole again.

Holy Spirit, reach into my life with Your Word.
Search out the places where sin hides, and remove
it from my life.

"AFTER YOU!" "NO, AFTER YOU!"

Do nothing out of selfish ambition or vain conceit,
but in humility consider others better than yourselves.

PHILIPPIANS 2:3

I t took me a long time to figure out why Mom and Dad have such a happy marriage," Gail told her brother. "Finally, I decided it's because they must have Philippians 2:3 as their watchword. They're so humble with each other."

Good marital relationships are founded on a kind of reciprocal-care agreement. Instead of looking out for personal interests and then considering the spouse, each partner of a successful couple puts aside selfishness and puts the other first. Neither gets cheated when both have that attitude.

One member doesn't constantly knuckle under to the other, fear offending the other, or give up every scrap of identity. None of those concepts fits Paul's description.

This verse isn't just for marriages. Any relationship becomes a blessing when people mutually care for each other. Imagine what churches would be like if Christians treated each other this way!

Whether it's another church member, a date, or a spouse, help me to put
others first, Lord. I want to let them know they're loved.

THE ULTIMATE PAYBACK: KINDNESS

Make sure that nobody pays back wrong for wrong,
but always try to be kind to each other and to everyone else.

1 THESSALONIANS 5:15

But you don't know what he did to me!" or, "You don't
know how she hurt me!" How often people say or think
these words as justification for getting back at someone
who hurt them badly. The implication always follows that they
have a right to retaliate. Our desire to even the score runs strong
when we've been done wrong.

But it isn't the best way. When we seek our own justice, we
forget how it pales before God's justice. If we leave wrongs in
His hands, pray for our abusers, and wait, wonderful things can
happen.

Instead of starting a long-term feud, make peace with your
enemy. He may turn into a friend. But if God brings down His
own justice, it will be better than yours ever could be.

Be kind to those who hurt you. Either way, you can't lose.

Father God, thank You that Your justice is far greater than mine. When
I'm wronged, let me leave the outcome of the situation in Your hands.

THE MOST IMPORTANT FRACTION: 1/10

Give, and it shall be given unto you;
good measure, pressed down, and shaken together,
and running over, shall men give into your bosom.

LUKE 6:38 KJV

*Y*ou want me to what? Jake didn't say it, but he might as well have. His Sunday school teacher could see the thought on his face. As they continued discussing tithing, Jake didn't say much—his body language spoke for him. He crossed his arms and waited.

Finally Jake said, "Ten percent? I already give to God when I can afford it, and I do lots of things for the church. Isn't that enough?"

Stinginess with God really doesn't hurt Him. He already owns all creation. We only hurt ourselves when we try to bargain God down to 9 percent, 8 percent. . .and then point out our own good points to make up for our lack of giving.

God wants to give to a generous giver. But He can't give to you if you hold your cash tightly to your chest. How can you take, when your hands are full?

Are your hands wide open today?

Lord, help me to understand Your blessing of giving. I want to be generous and openhearted to You.

A Good Character

Who can find a virtuous woman? for her price is far above rubies.

PROVERBS 31:10 KJV

When you date someone, do you look for the best-looking girl around, the guy with the most money—or a person with good character?

Dreams of your future spouse probably include a great-looking person, romantic evenings together, and wonderful conversations. You may not imagine a man who's truthful or a woman who treats her parents with respect.

God doesn't say you can't marry a good-looking mate or even one with a hefty bank account. But you could live without them. You can't live happily with a weak character.

Character doesn't look glamorous. You can't show off by sending your friend a picture of it. But you can live with it for a happy lifetime. You'll never worry where your mate is when you know he's trustworthy. You'll never fear a family get-together when you know she'll treat your parents kindly.

Is your date a noble character—or just a character?

Lord, character may not be the asset I'm dreaming of, but I know it's important. Turn my heart toward someone with a strong love for You and the willingness to do right.

MADE TO SERVE

I praise you because I am fearfully and wonderfully made;
your works are wonderful.

PSALM 139:14

I f all humanity worked for years on it, we'd never create a wonder like the human body. Imagine designing various body-part cells, each working smoothly and reproducing its very own sort. How much time would it take to make every atom of a healthy body work in sync with the others?

God created all this—and more—just out of His head. No laboratory, no special equipment; the Creator's mind alone worked it out in amazing detail, made it, and set this "invention" in an equally marvelous world.

When people try to tell you that everything in our universe "just happened," it's time to ask questions. Wouldn't it have taken a mighty intelligence, not just "accident," to plan all this?

But it's not just the universe—you are wonderfully created, made to a special design, with your own fingerprints, face, and body chemistry. On top of that, God says you're wonderful.

Shouldn't something so wonderful serve Him?

Lord, I don't think of myself as wonderful most days. I praise You for taking such care over my design. Use me for Your kingdom's business.

Maybe, Maybe Not

I hate double-minded men, but I love your law.

Psalm 119:113

Have you ever run into a double-minded person? It can drive you nuts!

A double-minded person believes one thing— until another person tries to sway him. Then he changes his mind. If a friend is double-minded, you'll always wonder if he will meet you when he said he will, support the cause he said he would help with, or move somewhere else on the spur of the moment. You'll never know what's up!

Double-minded people don't have a guide they follow consistently. If public opinion changes, so do they. Disapproval from a family member may sway them—today.

That's no way to live. Everyone needs to have certain standards, codes of conduct, and personal rules.

God's laws give us the guidelines we need to avoid double-mindedness. When we know what's wrong, we won't do it, even if public opinion says it's right. If a friend doesn't agree with us, we'll know why we won't change our minds. We're single-minded.

Lord, I don't want to sway in the breeze on every issue. Keep me firm in Your Word so I know Your laws.

It's Only a Box of Pencils!

"Shall I acquit a man with dishonest scales,
with a bag of false weights?"

MICAH 6:11

God takes wrongdoing seriously—much more seriously than we're likely to do.

Sometimes we'd like to fudge a little. Maybe we take a box of pencils from work and excuse ourselves with the idea that we do work at home once in a while, and we'll need them. We think we don't harm anyone if we take that little extra. We slide it behind our backs, and an hour later it doesn't bother us.

But it bothers God just as much as it bothered Him that the merchants of Judah were shortchanging customers. They used lighter weights, which meant less product for the customers and more money for them.

God is so holy that He can't ignore wrongdoing. Mismeasuring their goods was just a sign of the evil that lived in the merchants' hearts. They were more caught up in their profit than their love for God.

Don't ask God to ignore your sin. He'd be disregarding the love that's missing in your heart.

Thank You, Lord, that You don't leave me in my sin, even
when it only seems to weigh as much as a box of pencils.

THE IMPORTANCE OF TODAY

I know how to live on almost nothing or with everything.
I have learned the secret of living in every situation,
whether it is with a full stomach or empty, with plenty or little.

PHILIPPIANS 4:12 NLT

No one knows what the future will bring. Some struggle their whole lives with no visible signs of success for their efforts, while others zoom to the top and stay there. Most of us bounce around a lot, finding success in some things and failure in others.

Some people literally wish their lives away. "In six months, I'll get a raise," they say, blowing off the days between now and then as if they were unimportant. Why not have a good time in the present instead of wasting those six months? The raise may or may not come, but today is here for the taking and will never come again.

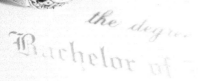

Father, teach me not to waste any of my life while I wait
for things to get better, to take each day as it comes and
enjoy it to the fullest.

ARE YOU A CONTENT POT?

"Woe to him who quarrels with his Maker."

ISAIAH 45:9

I t's a good thing this verse doesn't say "Woe to him who complains to his Maker," or we'd all be in trouble. As it is, we often skate on pretty thin ice, because quarreling, complaining, and moaning and groaning are all a little too close for comfort.

Why doesn't God "fix" the things that are wrong in our lives?

The Bible tells us we're just the clay He works with, and how often does a pot complain to the potter? "I'd like to be a little thinner, if you don't mind." It's a stupid idea, because the potter makes what he needs, and the clay has no voice in the creation. What does the clay know about the potter's needs and plans?

In the end, we and everything else in the world are whatever God wants us to be, and arguing about it is a waste of time and energy. Be the best pot you can be, and leave the rest to the Potter.

Father, I trust Your plans for me and my world. I don't know enough to argue about it, and it's not my place to do so. Forgive me when I become impatient.

Exercise Your Body
and Your Spirit

Everyone who competes in the games goes into strict training.
They do it to get a crown that will not last;
but we do it to get a crown that will last forever.

D o you work out to keep your body in decent shape? It takes a lot of determination and effort, but you keep at it because you know it will result in a longer, healthier life. Of course, in time your body will still fail, no matter how hard you train. There's no way around that, but you do everything you can to put it off a little longer.

What about your spiritual training? Do you give an equal amount of time and energy to that? Do you study the Bible, your spiritual training Manual, and obey its commands? Do you take advantage of the personal trainers who are willing to help you at no charge? When you get in spiritual shape, do you help others with their training?

Physical training can only take you so far. Spiritual training is for eternity.

Lord, don't let me ignore the fitness of my soul, which is far more important in the long run than the fitness of my body.

I Love You. . .You Love Me

"The LORD your God is with you, he is mighty to save.
He will take great delight in you, he will quiet you with his love,
he will rejoice over you with singing."

ZEPHANIAH 3:17

W hat's your first reaction to this verse?

"Who, me?" It's a little mind-boggling, isn't it? The Lord wants to save you from your enemies, just as He did for David. He takes delight in you—you make Him smile. When you're upset, His love will calm you. And when you come to Him, He will sing a song of joy.

The Bible's not talking about a group of people, either. It's talking about you, with all your fears and all your faults. With all the billions of people in this world, all the stars in the sky, all the other forms of life here or elsewhere, God is not too busy for you. When you fall in love, God is happy with you. When you have a child, He rejoices with you. When you suffer, He suffers. When you laugh, He laughs.

How do you repay love like that? The only way you can—with love.

Father, thank You for Your unbounded love. I know I am unworthy, but I am so grateful You care so much for me.

WANT SUCCESS? WORK HARD

"From everyone who has been given much, much will be demanded;
and from the one who has been entrusted with
much, much more will be asked."

LUKE 12:48

W
ho would complain if they suddenly found themselves rich or were promoted to positions of responsibility? Not too many of us. Everyone loves the idea of a windfall, but the truth is, your work has just begun when you see your dreams fulfilled.

When you have nothing, no one expects very much from you. Someone who stocks shelves is not expected to worry about the quality of the merchandise or the foreign exchange rate, but if a shelf stocker is suddenly put in charge of purchasing, he has to scramble to learn everything that goes with the new job and how to handle his new responsibilities.

None of that is bad or to be avoided, as long as you realize there's no such thing as a free lunch. Success comes from hard work and leads to even harder work.

Father, help me remember that it'll be a long time before I can rest on my laurels in this world. The more I have, the more will be required of me.

An Honest Legacy

A good name is more desirable than great riches;
to be esteemed is better than silver or gold.

PROVERBS 22:1

L ife offers us a lot of opportunities to cheat and get away with it. Creative cheaters can bluff their way into amazing salaries, high public office, or tax refunds large enough to support a small nation, and they seem to get away with it most of the time.

When they do, it's not always because they're so clever that no one notices. Sometimes, the people around them are perfectly aware of the cheating going on—but for reasons of their own, they look the other way. But they usually know who's a cheat, and they would never trust those people with much of value.

The next time you're tempted to cheat a little, ask yourself if it's worth the consequences. What would you prefer to see on your tombstone? "Here lies an honest man," or "He was successful, but. . ."?

Father, there are many ways to get to the top. Help me choose the ones that earn me the respect of others, even if the path is a little longer and harder.

GOD, THE ONLY TRUE SOURCE

"Do not turn to mediums or seek out spiritists,
for you will be defiled by them. I am the LORD your God."

LEVITICUS 19:31

You can talk to a psychic today through a 900 number instead of having to travel to the top of a faraway mountain. Isn't progress wonderful? Instant sin! For free.

The world has always had people willing to tell fortunes, give advice, or put the gullible in touch with their past lives. Some of them seem to give sensible advice, and if you read their books, they can give you a good feeling about yourself—something that's hard to find in the real world—but that's about all.

Some of these people claim to be prophets speaking for God. How can you deal with that? Well, the truth is, there hasn't been much work for prophets since Christ came on the scene, so skepticism is always in order.

If you need a peek into your future, why not go to the source? Ask God. Sometimes you will get an answer, sometimes you won't, but at least you can trust those answers you get. Don't dirty yourself with spiritualism that is not based on the Lord your God.

Father, teach me to seek my answers from You, not from anyone else.

YOU ARE GOD'S TEMPLE

"Do not cut your bodies for the dead
or put tattoo marks on yourselves. I am the LORD."

LEVITICUS 19:28

Tattoos are in, not to mention body piercing and other forms of personal mutilation. Some see them as personal statements: "It's my body, and I'll do what I like with it."

Sorry, folks, but it's not your body. "Do not offer the parts of your body to sin, as instruments of wickedness, but rather offer yourselves to God, as those who have been brought from death to life; and offer the parts of your body to him as instruments of righteousness" (Romans 6:13).

When you ask God to take care of your soul, your body is part of the deal. You are all His, and He does not want mutilated sacrifices. Your body is God's temple. He lives in you and through you, and you should no more desecrate that temple than you should take an ax to an altar.

Father, fads and fashions should never make me present a less-than-perfect sacrifice to You. Give me the strength I need to avoid anything that lessens my dedication to You.

Am I in Control?

Encourage the young men to be self-controlled.

TITUS 2:6

Ever since potty training, you've been learning self-control, and by now you're pretty sick of it. You have to control yourself on dates, at work, while driving or eating. Even your thoughts need to be controlled most of the time. Does it ever end?

Nope. But it does change. You get older, and self-control is easier. Not so many rampaging hormones, for one thing. You develop more consideration for others and tend to fly off the handle less frequently. Eventually you find the perfect balance point between your desires and civilization's expectations, and it's at that point that you become truly productive and fulfilled.

You can control yourself or let society control you, and society is a lot rougher on you. A lack of self-control will cost you jobs, love, and even jail time. When looked at logically, learning self-control is the easy way out.

Father, give me self-control when I need it, and teach me how to develop it on my own, so I can be a productive member of society and not endanger others to satisfy myself.

No Laughing Matter

Rejoice not when thine enemy falleth,
and let not thine heart be glad when he stumbleth:
lest the LORD see it, and it displease him,
and he turn away his wrath from him.

Proverbs 24:17–18 KJV

Here's an interesting angle on why we shouldn't clap when our enemies suffer. Our natural tendency is to be happy when the bully finally hits the playground dirt or the dictator disappears some dark night. He has gotten away with it for too long, and we rejoice when he gets his due.

But God knows the bully and the dictator. One day, His wrath will fall on them, without any help from us. He also doesn't want any cheering from the sidelines, any self-righteous gloating, any songs of joy—even ones that are hidden in our hearts. If He hears them, He will disapprove of them and turn away His wrath before the job is done. God respects everyone, good or bad, and expects us to do the same. We may not always love our enemies the way God commands, but we don't have to show joy at anyone's downfall.

Father, sometimes it's hard to respect those who don't respect me, but justice is Your job, not mine. Teach me how to love my enemies as You command.

Test Time!

Examine yourselves, whether ye be in the faith;
prove your own selves.

2 Corinthians 13:5 kjv

Oh, no, not another test! And it's not even going to be multiple choice.

Still, a little introspection is always a good idea. At least, you'll know how far off the mark you've wandered. So what are the criteria here? Who gets an A, and who fails?

First of all, this is an open-book test. Take your Bible and read all of Matthew. Read every word Jesus spoke and every command He ever gave. Point by point, how did you come out? Give yourself a grade on every command.

It could be kind of dismal until you hit Matthew 22:37–39: "'Love the Lord your God with all your heart and with all your soul and with all your mind.' This is the first and greatest commandment. And the second is like it: 'Love your neighbor as yourself.'"

Now throw away your entire test. This is the only question that counts. By the way, the person doing the grading is you, and you can grade on a curve. Not so hard, was it?

Father, in a real test, I'm sure I'd fail, but You forgive me and only require my love. I can do that.

GOD IS MY EMPLOYER

Whatever you do, work at it with all your heart,
as working for the LORD, not for men,
since you know that you will receive an inheritance
from the LORD as a reward.
It is the LORD Christ you are serving.

COLOSSIANS 3:23–24

Are you miserable in your job? Mentally switch employers—imagine you work for God, not your boss.

Once you decide to work as if God were your boss, everything changes. You can't call in sick every Monday when God knows every healthy cell in your body. You can't give less than your best to God, who knows exactly how capable you are and wants to reward your efforts. If it takes fifty hours a week to get the job done, would you complain to God?

A few months of this and your human supervisor is going to notice the change. You're getting the job done without resentment. Maybe you can be trusted, even promoted. She won't have the vaguest idea of what's come over you, but she'll be pleased, and supervisors who are pleased often turn into decent people. Try it.

Father, help me do all my work as if I were working for You, no matter how bad conditions are for me.

MAKING THE RIGHT CHOICES

Finish your outdoor work and get your fields ready;
after that, build your house.

PROVERBS 24:27

This verse speaks of a basic survival situation most of us never have to face, but it has a modern parallel. Money is scarce when you're young. The little extra you have can be invested in a decent apartment or a course that will help you in your work. Isn't it better to take the course and live in a shoe-box apartment for a year? A new apartment won't give you any return on your investment, but new skills will have immediate results, securing your livelihood.

Life is full of hard choices, and waiting for future rewards is not easy, but a little effort in the right places can make all the difference in the world.

Father, help me make the right choices in where I invest my money and my work, even if it means I have to give up some things I want very much.

I'm Not Perfect,
You're Not Perfect

So God created man in his own image,
in the image of God he created him;
male and female he created them. God blessed them.

GENESIS 1:27–28

Y ou were created in God's image. God made you in a
special design and blessed you.

But that special creation and blessing aren't yours
alone. He also created and blessed the person you'll marry. Are
you ready to treat your spouse as a person God has blessed? Do
you remember that in His eyes you're both important? Can you
keep each other from sin and encourage each other in your faith?

When you marry someone you know is created in God's
image and realize just what that means, you don't mistreat your
spouse. Though you may disappoint each other sometimes, you
remember that this God-created person is special—not perfect.
Sin may mar God's creation, but it cannot change the value of
His work.

A believing man and wife are blessed by God. Even the most
challenging life situations can't change that promise.

Jesus, I want to treat my spouse like a treasure from You. Help me see
when I'm ready for the blessing of marriage.

LEARN FROM YOUR MISTAKES

Pride only breeds quarrels,
but wisdom is found in those who take advice.

PROVERBS 13:10

"Mr. Milton drives me crazy," Lisa admitted to a coworker. "Every other day, he's criticizing my work. I almost snapped back at him."

Criticism isn't easy to take. At first, your mind wants to snap back with explanations and countercriticisms. *Well, if I'd had enough time. . . If I'd gotten the right information. . .*

Maybe your objections are true, but giving a sharp answer won't help others appreciate your efforts. Pride can get in the way of good work.

When you are criticized, take a good look at the critique. Were you sloppy? Could you have done better? What would have helped you improve? Don't start with excuses, but look at it from your boss's point of view. Would you like your work if you were the boss?

If you've made mistakes, learn from them. Turn the critique into advice that helps you do better.

I know I'm not perfect, God, but sometimes it's hard to admit it to my boss. Keep our communication clear so pride can't lead us into quarrels.

Look Out! There's a Hole!

He also told them this parable:
"Can a blind man lead a blind man?
Will they not both fall into a pit?"

What a delightful description Jesus gave us in this parable. You can easily see this pair ending up in a pit, because neither can see the road.

Sometimes we're no better than these foolish men. Without even thinking of it, we hang on to someone who's going in the wrong direction. By the time we realize we've been following others, not God, we're on the edge of a crater.

Want to know if you will end in a spiritual hole? Look at the people you follow. Are they filled with peace and serving God, or are they running their own show, constantly dissatisfied with life?

Since you'll end up much like the people you follow most, be sure the people you emulate are worth following. Do they do what the Bible says is right? Are they honest and loving?

In the end, make sure you're following the greatest Leader—Jesus. His paths don't go into pits.

Lord, I want to be a leader who won't bring others into a pit. Guide me this day to walk in Your footsteps.

WISDOM FOR THE GRADUATE   177

SAME TIME, SAME PLACE

The Israelites ate manna forty years. . .
until they reached the border of Canaan.

EXODUS 16:35

You might call it "doing laps." Just as a swimmer goes back and forth in the pool to build up strength, sometimes God keeps us in the same place, doing the same thing, for a long time.

The Israelites complained that they didn't have food, so God gave them manna. . .today and tomorrow and the next day. Boy, were they sick of that white, waferlike stuff! Like the swimmer in the pool, they never got anything different.

In our spiritual walk, when we get stuck "doing laps," we need to take a look at ourselves. Maybe, like the Israelites, we've sinned, and God is trying to humble us. Or maybe we need to gain strength, so God has us exercising the same spiritual muscle over and over again.

If you're doing laps, search your heart. Do you need to confess some sin so you can move on? If not, don't get discouraged. God is building up your strength.

That's why you're diving into the water one more time.

Lord, when I feel waterlogged, show me why I'm diving into the water again.

Following the Rules

As ye have always obeyed, not as in my presence only,
but now much more in my absence,
work out your own salvation with fear and trembling.

PHILIPPIANS 2:12 KJV

Now that you are on your own, it's easy to think, *Mom and Dad aren't here to yell at me. I'll just do things my way.* Well, when it comes to how you vacuum your apartment, it doesn't matter if you don't obey Mom and Dad's rules, as long as things get clean. But moral choices do matter.

Mom and Dad might not be there at midnight, when you have to decide whether or not to invite your date to your apartment for "a cup of coffee." But soon you'll find you won't just be doing the wrong thing on your date, you'll be lying about how you spent the weekend.

Whether or not Paul was there, the Philippians toed the line morally. Perhaps they understood that they weren't obeying Paul, but God. Paul wasn't being a rule maker. He showed them the best way to have a terrific relationship with God. They wanted that, so they followed the "rules."

Father God, sometimes Your ways seem so restrictive. I need to remember they're leading me to a happier, more holy life.

Avoid Boasters

Why do you boast of evil, you mighty man?
Why do you boast all day long,
you who are a disgrace in the eyes of God?

Psalm 52:1

You're working hard, trying to be honest, even though you don't get a large salary and could really use a few things. Then a coworker boasts to someone else about a killing he made by doing wrong.

Why him and not me? you may wonder.

Don't follow him. First, chances are you can't duplicate what he's done. You're likely to get caught if you try to repeat the same slick deal.

But even if you could repeat his method and no one caught you, it wouldn't be worth the price. When you decided to pray, you'd feel disgrace taking up space between you and God. You'd wonder if He was listening very closely. Should you escape that quiet time without confessing the sin, you'd start feeling uncomfortable, so you'd pray less often.

Soon you wouldn't pray at all, and your church attendance would start slipping.

Don't listen to those who boast of evil; instead, do some of your own boasting in the God who saved you.

Turn me back from sin, Lord. Close my ears to sinners' boasting.

A MATTER OF FAITH

Now faith is being sure of what we hope for
and certain of what we do not see.

HEBREWS 11:1

A m I crazy to believe in this? Has that thought ever run through your mind when you were thinking about the Virgin Birth, Moses and the burning bush, or the Resurrection?

Logically, these events don't seem to make much sense. After all, each was a one-time incident that no one can re-create. Many question the truth of these biblical accounts.

In some circles, people have become so doubtful that they try to explain away these phenomena. But such would-be Christians have missed the point, haven't they? Of course none of these events can be explained. It's a matter of faith, not intellectual "sight."

As we exercise our faith, even though we can't work out exactly how such things happened, we can begin to see how it's all part of God's plan.

Then we're believing in Jesus.

Lord, I praise You for being so marvelous and powerful that You boggle my mind. Help me trust in Your power. I want to walk by faith.

LISTEN TO YOUR FATHER

Now therefore hearken, O Israel,
unto the statutes and unto the judgments, which I teach you,
for to do them, that ye may live, and go in and possess the land
which the LORD God of your fathers giveth you.

DEUTERONOMY 4:1 KJV

Do you avoid obeying God's Word and only approach Him when you need something?

If so, you probably struggle in your Christian walk. Seeing God as a sort of "celestial Santa Claus" shows a selfishness that separates you from God's blessing.

The nation of Israel followed God when it was convenient. They got a blessing—the Promised Land—but only on a forty-year revised schedule.

Obey God because you love Him and want to be more like Him, and He gives you your Promised Land immediately, not forty years later. His blessings are real, but not automatic.

God's giving isn't tit-for-tat—it's all-out sharing from a Father who loves children who listen to Him. But He can't reward disobedient children.

So listen to your Father.

Father, I know You want to bless me. Keep me from sin that ruins blessing.

I Need Patience. . .Quick!

*"Let God weigh me in honest scales
and he will know that I am blameless."*

JOB 31:6

Job seemed to have everything—a happy family, lots of money, and a great relationship with God. Who wouldn't envy him?

Until disaster struck.

Suddenly Job was scratching his sores, sitting atop a dunghill, without a supportive family—and with friends like his, no one needed an enemy! Where had Job gone wrong? Hadn't he been honest with everyone he'd dealt with? He hadn't made his millions by walking over others. This honest man cried out to God.

But God didn't seem to answer.

We know. We've tried our best at work, but we get laid off. We're honest with our money, but someone else takes his girl to a play, while we go to the park. We pray, but nothing changes.

Has God forgotten us? No way! The answer may not come overnight—it didn't for Job. But in the end, blessing overwhelmed him. God does that for us, too. Sometimes, the more time He takes to develop a blessing, the better it is.

When Your blessings come slowly, keep me patient, Lord.

HAPPILY EVER AFTER

A man will. . .be united to his wife, and they will become one flesh.

GENESIS 2:24

And they lived happily ever after." Deep down inside, every couple would like this tribute to apply to their marriage. Even if you're still single, you probably imagine yourself finding Mr. or Ms. Right.

No one gets married to experience the pain of divorce. But about half of American marriages end that way. So you may ask, *Can I be sure it'll work for me?*

Marital guarantees don't exist. You can't know that hard times will never hit you—everyone has them. But a marriage God puts together can be even better than the "happily ever after" variety, because in a God-made marriage, happiness doesn't depend on circumstances.

Real marital unity comes when two people count on the commitment they made before God and trust Him to pull them through any problem. It's amazing what they can experience and still stay together. Their happiness in each other comes from God, not their own power. So the more they turn to Him, the stronger their marriage grows.

You can have a God-made marriage. Just ask Him for one, and wait for His timing.

Thank You, Lord, that You, not a storyteller, put marriages together.

No Longer a Stranger

Thou shalt neither vex a stranger, nor oppress him:
for ye were strangers in the land of Egypt.
EXODUS 22:21 KJV

You move to a new town or a new school, and for the first few days you feel really strange. You don't know where to go for anything you need. You don't know whom to ask for advice.

Then someone comes along and tells you about some good stores, the best bank, and maybe a great doctor. All of a sudden, you're beginning to find your feet. You feel more secure, and life balances out again.

God knows what it feels like to be in a strange place (after all, didn't Jesus leave His home to come to earth?). He understands that sometimes you have to go to a new place (didn't He call Abram to move?).

Maybe because of that, He tells us to have compassion for the new person on the block. We don't need to wonder if we should stretch out a welcoming hand. God has been there before us, greeting the outcast.

Thank You, Lord, for caring for me when I'm in a new place. Help me to reach out to others who are feeling strange in a new town, a new job, or a new country.

How Long Is Forever?

*"For God so loved the world that he gave his one and only Son,
that whoever believes in him shall not perish but have eternal life."*

John 3:16

"Eternal life"—have you ever thought of time without end,
stretching on and on? But not dull, useless hours or
overly hectic days—time for God's kind of life that's
continually fresh and exciting without being rushed.

Most of us can rattle off John 3:16 without even thinking
about it. But have we thought about what we'll do with endless
life with the Creator of the universe?

If we listed everything we'd like to do in heaven, most of us
would have trouble filling up a month, much less eternity. From
an earthly point of view, we can imagine boredom setting in early.

But living in the home of "new life" leaves no room for
boredom. Scripture only gives us faint glimpses, but certainly a
Father who took such efforts to save us wouldn't skimp
on our shared eternity.

No matter what we do in heaven, God will be
bigger than our wildest dreams.

*Lord, when I think of time without limits, my mind
goes fuzzy. I only know I want to glorify You
with every atom of my being.*

God's Plan or Your Plans?

For that ye ought to say,
If the LORD will, we shall live, and do this, or that.

JAMES 4:15 KJV

W hat does James mean in this verse?" Kirsten asked. "Sounds as if he's saying we should never make plans. If I did that, my life'd be a mess!"

Her Bible study leader explained that God wasn't frowning on our making plans. But He doesn't want us to get caught up in our plans and never look to Him for guidance. Planning done without God leads down a dead-end street.

Maybe lots of options vie for your attention: Should you move in with friends, take a job in another state, or start dating someone new?

Though you see the exciting changes ahead, you don't have a God's-eye view of your life. He sees the big picture and wants to help you make the right choices.

So why not ask Him what the next step is?

My days need to be filled, Lord. Let them overflow with Your will for me.

REGRET A MISTAKE?
FORGET ABOUT IT!

Forgetting what is behind and straining toward what is ahead,
I press on toward the goal to win the prize
for which God has called me heavenward in Christ Jesus.

PHILIPPIANS 3:13–14

Look back, and you can see some things you wish you hadn't done—and some good things you never found time for. Maybe you made a career choice that's not so great, or you had some wonderful friends with whom you lost touch.

Don't wallow in your past mistakes—jump beyond them. There are few things in life that you can't change, if you're willing to spend time and effort on them.

Sure, rewriting your resume and contacting companies isn't your favorite free-time project. But your new job might be worth it. Calling a friend might be hard to fit into your schedule—and you might get his answering machine a few times—but imagine rekindling the faith you shared last summer!

Paul knew that moving ahead spiritually meant forgetting past mistakes and moving on. You can do that!

Lord, I thank You for what You've brought me through. Help me move ahead in faith.

Scripture Index

Old Testament